A Puppy Dies

and other stories from the
Holy Land

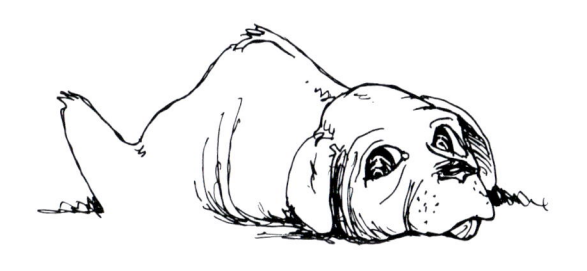

TIMOTHY BILES

© Timothy Biles
ISBN No. 0 9517915 6 7

Printed by Creeds the Printers, Broadoak, Bridport, Dorset DT6 5NL

ACKNOWLEDGEMENTS

The author is grateful to

MYRTLE GILDERSLEVE
*who typed the original manuscript with great care
and suffered all the alterations with matching patience*

JOHN ANDERSON
*whose line drawings complemented the text
and brought smiles 'midst the sorrows*

JOAN BILES
*who provided many of the photographs and designed
the cover with John Anderson*

HUGH MOWAT
who provided the photograph on page 56

Cover picture: Soldiers of the occupying army view the Old City from the top of the Damascus Gate.

This book is dedicated to all who suffer injustice

INTRODUCTION

12th August 1983

A Puppy Dies

It might have been hit by a car, because it lay on a footpath, blood coming out somewhere at the back where the leg was twisted.

I moved her to a pile of leaves and laid her there. She wasn't more than ten weeks old. I tickled her under her chin. The neck was so scraggy – about the size of my forefinger. I was sure she was dying.

Her brown eyes looked into mine and I thought – if we were in England, something could be done. We'd get a vet. He'd save her. The 'Echo' would publish a photograph. *"Ten week old puppy saved by Vicar,"* and twenty people would want her. It would all end happily. The English love their dogs, especially one down on its luck. But here, in Jerusalem, it is another story. Suppose I take it to the hotel? They will think me mad – worrying about a dog. Too many bark at night, roam the streets, overturn the dustbins. Suppose I give it to an Arab passing by? They've too many mouths to feed already. They can't pay their bills as it is, and they haven't a telephone to get a vet. It's hopeless. It will die. So I left it on its pile of leaves, and walked on, to Gethsemane.

The Jerusalem night sky was blacker than black, but the white floodlights brilliantly revealed the City walls tessellated, as if for battle. And inside the walls rose the Golden Dome, in all its splendour, and the dome of the Holy Sepulchre, centres of strife for more than a thousand years. The traffic rushed by, noisily. Armoured lorries were grinding up the hill, bound for Lebanon, tourists were speeding down the hill – no need to get out of their taxis as long as they got their photographs!

In the rocky garden at Gethsemane, crickets chirruped and two tethered goats stirred. They nuzzled me, seeking affection, enjoying human company and the cool evening air. I listened to the traffic. It spoke of strife. I looked at the City walls and they spoke of battle, and I recalled the scripture read in church the previous Sunday. *"I am sending you to a people of hard face and stubborn heart, but I will make your forehead hard against their forehead, like adamant harder than flint."*

Yes, this is a hard land. But, today, the battle for it is no battle. One side has everything, the other nothing. The side which has the American aid has the wealth. The side which has the established government makes the laws. The side which has the army takes the land – and with it the homes and the livelihood of the people.

In that Garden, I realised that it was not only a goat that looked for affection, but a people. In the Garden, I realised it was not only a puppy that was dying, but the Palestinian people, whose cries were unheard. That night, I walked back up the road to see the puppy. I looked at it. It fixed those brown eyes on me and whimpered. There was nothing I could do. I returned to the comfort of my hotel.

Next morning, Israeli jets flew over. It was the daily show of strength. The tanks were still lumbering up the hill, under the City walls. And the puppy was dead.

I buried it, in Gethsemane.

Chapter One

The Mount of Olives

15th August, 1983

Islamic Angels

It could not possibly have been any hotter. If it had been any hotter, even by a single degree, Jerusalem would have gone up in flames, swallowed by a fireball. People had said that because Jerusalem was "a city built on a hill", 1,300 feet above sea level, it was always the coolest spot in the Holy Land. Not today! The desert wind, known in Hebrew as the ruarch, the destroyer, was blowing. It was a wind that burned everything in its path. The blasts were coming, wave upon wave, relentlessly. It was as if the oven door had been left open and no one could close it.

"Go to the top of the Mount of Olives," someone said. "It's the highest point and the coolest." It also has the most breath-taking panoramic view, looking across the Kidron Valley to the Holy City. When the pilgrims of ancient times, Jesus included, went up to Jerusalem "to keep the feast" their journey from Jericho would have led them to the top of the Mount of Olives and to the sight of the Holy City spread before them. Little wonder they sang *"I will lift up mine eyes to the hills, from whence cometh my strength"* as they made their way. And when they reached the top and saw the city, it was no wonder they sang again *"I was glad when they said unto me, we will go into the House of the Lord"*. And it was from that same hillside that Jesus prepared to enter the Holy City on the first Palm Sunday, seated on a donkey, the beast of burden. It was there that he lamented for the people of Jerusalem. *"Oh! Jerusalem, Jerusalem, that killeth the prophets, if only you had known the ways of peace..."*

Yes, it would be a good thing to go to the top of the Mount of Olives and think on these things in the cool breeze which refreshes every hilltop. But of course, to reach the top it was necessary to start at the bottom, a lesson of life if ever there was one. And at the bottom, by the Garden of Gethsemene, the path looked stony and very steep, and in that cauldron the sun beat down, stronger than ever, it seemed.

It might have been wiser not to have started the climb because, after about twenty paces, fatigue took its toll. There was nowhere to sit or rest except in the midst of the stones. But all was worthwhile because the view which emerged was of Jerusalem the golden, the ancient walls golden in the sunlight and the golden dome peeping above them. A few more steps, backwards, facing the city and more of the golden dome rose into view. Spectacular! But no cooler. The salt sweat ran into my eyes and stung so much that I screwed them shut. So that is why heat is sometimes called blinding. By then I was about half-way up the Mount, and about half dead. It was time to give up and go down.

At that moment there came the sound of music. Had I died? Was it the heavenly host welcoming me? No, it was a small boy leading some goats across a field and playing his flute as he went. He and his goats passed me by and as I watched they went through a gate in the wall. It was tempting to follow but I had just decided to go down, not up, but within a minute the boy returned with a skin full of water. Everyone knows it's wise to check water and keep to the bottled variety, preferably from a fresh spring, but in my condition who cared? The boy signalled, so it was with renewed strength and interest that we went through the gateway in the wall and entered an olive grove. And there was a gardener watering trees and plants from a hosepipe. And there were water spouts, several of them, every ten yards or so. The boy turned one on and, kneeling down, drank plentifully. I followed. The gardener, an old and wizened sun-cracked soul, hosed his kaffiyeh (head dress) and wrapped it round my neck so that cold water ran down my back. Like nectar, it was the gift of the gods!

By then it was clear. We were in an olive grove above Gethsemene and we were looking straight into the Old City, the Golden Dome seemed almost within reach. A plaque told me, in French, that the garden commemorated the visit of Pope Paul VI to Jerusalem in 1964. The Garden was set apart as a place of prayer for Unity and Peace. It was a welcome and unexpected oasis on the steep and rugged pathway. No guide book had told me there was such a place. The discovery was due to a young goatherd and an old gardener. Two Moslems had lifted me out of despair and into a place of refreshment. God's angels come unawares.

May, 1984

The Shirt off your back

The 'Pope's Garden' on the Mount of Olives seems to be the ideal place for a little peace and quite. It provides an escape from the hubbub of the Old City, its busy markets, narrow alleys and constant noise. And yet the panoramic view keeps the Holy City, its problems and injustices inescapably in mind. The Garden invites prayer and encourages reflection and that was my peaceful purpose before the distraction.

The distraction came from two youths who enjoyed themselves kicking a plastic football until the 'muezzin', the Moslem call to prayer, rang out from the city's mosques. The two youths took off their shoes and socks and went through a form of ablutions, using the garden spray. Then one of them approached me and said "Excuzee me. We pray now. We have your shirt, pleeze." It was in my hand at the time, while the sun soaked me.

In England people had warned about such things. "Watch those Arabs. They'll have the shirt off your back" had been a common expression. "Watch those kids, the little beggars will follow you wherever you go," people had said. Now it was happening. They smoothed the shirt on the stones and prostrated themselves several times, head to the ground, their youthful bodies framed by the walled city, the Holy City. It was from this same hillside that Jesus had prostrated himself in the stony Garden in Gethsemene, when he had prayed until his sweat was as drops of blood. It was on this same mount that the disciples had asked "Lord, teach us to pray." So when the boys finished their prayers and returned the shirt, it was natural to ask them what they said in their prayers. "We pray that God is great, we pray that he will have mercy on all men. We pray that men live as brothers. We pray that peace will come in our land, as Allah wills." My sentiments exactly! Their prayers and mine, up to the distraction, were of one heart.

Then came the inevitable question, the mantra familiar to every traveller. "Where you from? What your name? How many children you have?" Six children is my standard lying reply. It makes a suitable impression and earns respect. A pity it's undeserved. "You Eengleesh," they said, "you like fish and chips. Come." So we climbed to the top of the Mount to enjoy the local equivalent, pitta bread filled with egg plant, bought from a street stall, less than a dollar for the three of us.

And the English advisers who had said "the little beggars will never leave you" were right. "We take you to Bethany ... we take you to camel man ... we take you home to tea…" and all these things we did, on successive days. But never to the new city, Jewish Jerusalem. "That is not good for us. My father taken to prison there. No, no, we not go."

On the last day it was time to say goodbye and to thank them for all their help, the guidance, the conversation. Mohammed and Mustafa had made me feel at home, they had put me on the right buses and they loved talking football. They supported Liverpool. It was a pity they had never heard of Southampton, though they did say "Kevin Keegan" many times, not knowing he played for the Saints.

My farewells had an unexpected sting in the tail. "No, no," they kept saying. They would accept no gifts. "No, no," they said. "You welcome in our land." It was not the picture English people had painted. Quite the reverse. In the end they accepted the shirt which had been their prayer mat, but they had to be persuaded.

In a strange and unexpected way the purpose of peace and reconciliation for which the Garden was set apart, had been fulfilled. Yet as I made my way down the hill, leaving them behind, I was filled with foreboding of what their future may hold.

22nd May, 1984

Seeing Stars

A surprising variety of people find their way into the "Pope's Garden" on the Mount of Olives. Today's surprise arrival was Father Thomas, a Benedictine monk from the Dormition Abbey, who arrived in a chauffer-driven limousine. He had come to complete a painting of the Old City, which included the Abbey. We fell into conversation because he was anxious about returning to the Abbey alone. He wanted "an escort" because he had a bad back and couldn't carry the easel. He was also worried about going through the Old City's alleys alone. He was afraid he would lose the way and, as his neck was also subject to seizures in which it got 'locked', he wouldn't be able to find the way, especially if he was carrying the easel. It was all a little mysterious because he wasn't much more than half my age and had lived in Jerusalem several years, certainly long enough to know the way better than an occasional visitor.

While we sat, he told me he was a specialist painter of icons and that his works were in Canterbury Cathedral, the French monastery of Bec, the Belgium community of Chevtogne and that he was working on something for the 'White Russians' who were preparing for the return of the Czar. It all seemed a little odd, but almost everything in this land is a little odd.

It all got a good deal odder when Father Thomas asked my date of birth and told me I was an Arian. "You are aggressive, athletic, used to bashing your head against a brick wall, and red is your favourite colour," he told me. "That is why I want you to protect me through the Old City." This didn't seem a very flattering personality portrait for a parish priest. Was there no place for gentleness, sympathy and compassion for an Arian? "It all depends on the position of the outer and inner planets when you are born," he answered, "and whether your star was in the ascendant." He regretted that the Christian church had abandoned its true heritage, the wisdom contained in ancient mythology. He blamed the historic watershed in the 2nd century when the church had rejected Gnosticism. "We should have absorbed it," said Father Thomas. "We closed the door on all manner of legitimate religious

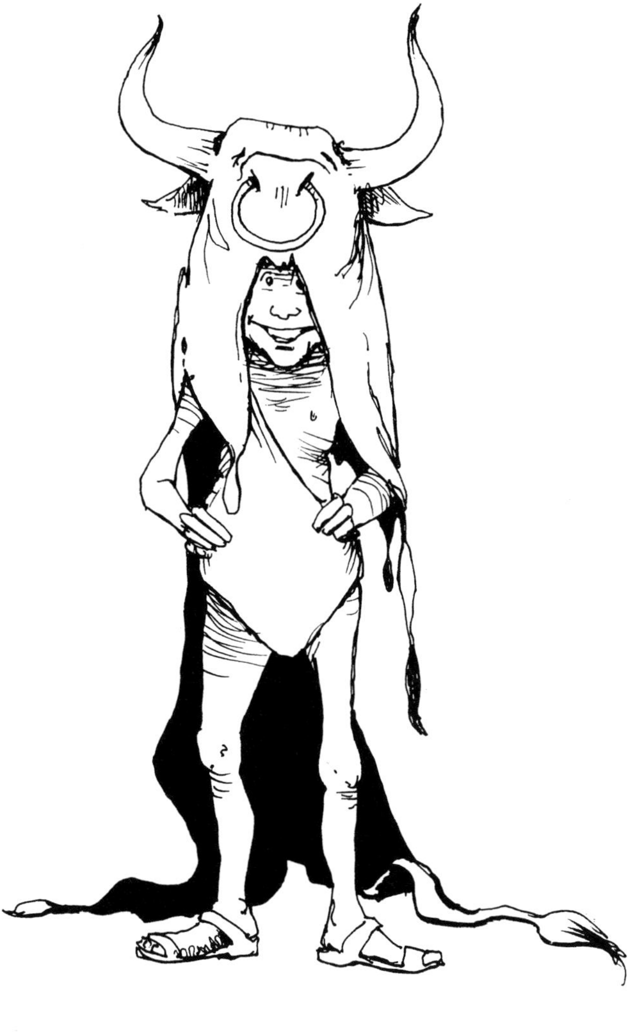

experience," he said. "We have exiled so much spirituality, now it hides in esoteric circles of the East. We must reclaim it!" It seemed to me that the banning of Gnosticism hadn't touched him, but these thoughts remained with me, silently, while a gentle smile was conjured up to suppress the Arian demon of aggression.

By the time we left the olive grove, this garden of peace and prayer, Father Thomas was hobbling rather badly and the pain was spreading to his neck so that he couldn't carry any of his painting equipment. In fact, as we ventured down the hill, gingerly, he couldn't turn his head to the left or the right. At the bottom of the hill, alongside Gethsemene, it was time to call a taxi. The responsibility of guiding him through the alleys of the Old City was too much, even if I am an Aries – aggressive, athletic and used to bashing my head against a wall, which I can not believe is the whole story.

Back at the monastery he invited me into the garden where we sat in the shade under an awning and he ordered a bottle of ice cool wine. "Rosé, the usual," he said to the boy, who brought it on a silver tray. A much older monk, leaning on a crutch, was working in the garden, doing some very demanding physical work and it occurred to me that he might justifiably be annoyed that this much younger monk was smoking, drinking wine and chatting in the cool of the garden, while he laboured. But Father Thomas assured me that for health reasons he had dispensation from work, so we continued to sup wine while he unfolded more reflections on the stars and their courses, until he felt his back trouble coming on again.

It was a mistake not to have asked him what star he was born under and how the planets lined up that day. I fear his star may not have been in the ascendant.

Saturday, 11th May, 1985

Prayers and Parties

No sooner had I settled in the Garden, to admire the scene than a group of Palestinians arrived and, with great excitement, started kindling a fire in the garden. There was even more excitement when they managed to get a 'gusher' from one of the water pipes, about three inches above ground level. One by one they got down on hands and knees, or into a 'press up' position to drink from the fountain. There was great hilarity when the fattest of them couldn't get low enough and got himself and his cigarettes soaked. It was like watching the clowns' interlude at the circus and I laughed heartily from my privileged view on the garden wall. Chicken legs were grilling and two large bottles of the local spirits (Arak) were adding to the party atmosphere. "Come and eat," said one of the group and they all waved me to join them. I was much in doubt, but remembered a maxim taught by an old priest many years ago "when in doubt, say 'yes.'" Many good things have come from that positive approach and so I clambered down off the wall and joined them.

We squatted on our haunches, knees near chins and, in no time at all, I was passed a chicken leg and a plastic tumbler of Arak. They munched and crunched the chicken legs noisily and then threw them over their shoulders, so I did the same and then was immediately passed another while the tumbler was refilled. One fellow spoke good English and I asked him where all the women were. "All at home," he said. "That's where they belong!" and they all laughed. They talked of their families and I gathered that most had sons in either America, Jordan, Paris, Leningrad or Australia. "There is no future here," he explained. Others, sadly, had sons in Lebanon while others did not know where their sons might be. "Syria, Iraq, who knows. Palestine is no more. Our sons go and we can only say God go with you, my son." Loaves of pitta bread came next, one each, and I noted that, before they ate them, they used them like little cloths to clean all the chicken fat and grease from their hands. I hadn't eaten as expertly as they had and the grease had run all the way to my armpits. I needed a shower but cleaned myself with the bread, as they had, and drank another tumbler of the strong spirit. By then, the fun of it all, the great heat and the Arak had got to me and I was laughing happily without quite knowing the joke. Eventually, they took to playing cards. "Loser pays for everything," they said, but mercifully they didn't expect me to stay for that, so I bade farewell with many thanks but it wasn't as easy to climb the wall as it had been an hour earlier. So I left the Holy Garden, set aside by the Pope as a place of prayer, with my legs like rubber and my steps uncertain. I sat in the shade of the first olive tree to recover myself, slightly guilty that I hadn't used the Garden for prayer. Then I hoped that the fun and the bonhomie had, in the sight of God, not been entirely out of tune with the Garden's theme of Peace and reconciliation among all God's people.

Monday, 13th May, 1985

The Garden is Dedicated

It was the day that the Garden of Peace on the Mount of Olives was to be dedicated. The ceremony was to be at 8.00am, a most awkward time for me as one hostel had turned me out by then but it was too early for the new one to take me in. It would have been a shame to miss the Dedication because the Garden's purpose is inspired and my enjoyment of its benefits is frequent. But to be there by 8.00 a.m. would mean lugging all my worldly goods up the Mount of Olives with me. This is where back-packs are such a blessing. Like a bosom friend, they stick with the traveller through thick and thin, they know what it is to bear another's burden, as the Gospel requires. Backpackers are too often looked upon with some suspicion, as if second class citizens. Yet there is something of the Gospel about them as they travel lightly around this world refusing the temptation to gather possessions. In fact at a recent hostel one back-packer, who was also a great reader, said he had solved the weight problem caused by books. After reading a page he immediately tore it out and ate it, so that as he journeyed his pack became lighter instead of heavier. It gave new meaning to the prayer which invites us to read, mark, learn and inwardly digest the Scriptures.

So it was a back-pack climb across the goat tracks to reach the Garden by 8.00am. The sun seemed strong already, the climb steeper than ever and the stony footholds kept slipping away. At some points it was a hands and knees effort. Goats do it so much better, they skip and look as if they are enjoying themselves. The climb took longer than expected and it was already 8.00am when I clambered over the garden wall.

What a surprise! The place had been transformed by rows and rows of white chairs, each bearing the name of an invited guest. There was the Archbishop of Paris, who had flown in especially for the occasion, the Prior of the Benedictines, the Superior of the Sisters of Sion, the French Consul, the entire Boegner family, the Papal legate, our own Bishop George Appleton with the Dean of our Cathedral. Four Benedictine monks arrived in a Mercedes and a whole fleet of limousines was lined up outside the iron gates.

The formality of it all took me by surprise, but there was an empty chair in the back row which seemed the best place for me. However, my route was blocked by a very smart uniformed steward who said "There is going to be a service." The implication was obvious – that a back-packer, and especially one who had arrived on foot and had climbed over the wall, was not welcome. I claimed the chair with some resolution and sat down firmly, thanking him for his information, but peeved on behalf of all back-packers.

The service was a succession of addresses by the various dignitaries. The Archbishop of Paris spoke in French for about twenty minutes and was followed by a Baptist from England who spoke for more than half an hour about the Ecumenical movement which for 20 years (1946-66) had been inspired by Marc Boegner but which had declined tragically in the twenty years since his death. Then Marc Boegner's son spoke of Pope Paul VI and his friendship with his father, a friendship which had influenced both men and had brought love among separated brethren.

Finally, came the Dedication Prayer which was introduced by Bishop George Appleton. He invited every priest or minister present to raise his arm and join in the ancient Aaronic blessing. This delighted me. To be included at this vital moment seemed a fulfilment. It was that gracious old gardener with the sun-cracked face and the little goat herd with his precious pouch of water who had introduced me to the place, two years ago. If only they had been there too! So my arm was raised for the blessing when, to my dismay, the smart steward rushed up and hissed "Priests! Priests! Only priests!" and tried to pull my arm down. I resisted and, gathering my strength, forced my arm higher, taking his with mine. Maybe he blessed it too.

Then it was time for the official photographs before the dignitaries sped off in their limousines to the Reception at the French Embassy and my backpack and I jumped over the wall, and made our way down the goat tracks.

Thursday, 16th May, 1985

The Goats have it!

Peace is in scarce supply in Jerusalem and so it seemed right on my last day of this visit to spend some time in the Peace Garden, on the Mount of Olives. However, a seat under an olive tree, with George Appleton's book of prayers for the Holy Land and that wonderful view of the City, did not provide the expected peace.

Three kid goats joined me. Their sleek shiny black coats spoke of good health and care. It was as if they had just been polished. And they frolicked in the most skittish way, kicking their back legs in the air as they went. And every time I threw a stick or a stone, they chased it and threw it in the air, as any puppy would at home. There was no food from me, but one started nibbling my hard-working trainers. That was not permissible, those trainers have seen me through desert walks and many rough places. They may look old and ugly and they may smell attractive to a young goat but they are precious to me, so the goat got a reproachful tap on the nose, whereupon it took George Appleton's prayers right out of my lap, tossed them in the air and went off to chew over a few pages. Meanwhile another started to nibble my hair and lick my neck with its sandpaper tongue. No doubt the salt was attractive.

So there was nothing for it but to abandon the Garden and move downhill, but they followed and another dozen or so joined them. Cutting across the fields was a foolish mistake, they were on their own territory and all their friends joined them. It was quite a worry as Gethsemene came into sight with its busy main roads by which time my following must have exceeded fifty, making me helpless and exposed in front of Gethsemene's crowds. What was my fatal charm, to a goat?

There was no option but to turn around, retrace my steps up that hot and stony path and hope they would follow, which they did. Was my charm in my smell? Was it richer than I knew? Perhaps this is why the Dean of the Cathedral, who is always immaculate, from slickly parted hair to finely polished shoes, had described me as "looking as if he has fallen from the trees". Eventually the goats returned to our meeting place and all that was left was for me to make my get-away. So I ran like mad for the big iron gates, which I normally do not use, and slammed them shut behind me. The last I saw of them they were digesting Bishop Appleton's prayers, contentedly.

Wednesday, 3rd September 1986

A Body Disturbs the Peace

The plan for the first day of this new tour was to keep things simple and enjoy a peaceful renewal of old friendships. It would also be good to meet the new Dean of our Cathedral and avoid exertion in the heat which contrasted so greatly with the dull misery of the cold wet August left behind.

The Dean hadn't appeared at breakfast so that part of the plan didn't work, and another disappointment awaited in the Old City. My friend, Fareidah, of the Arts Benevolent Centre, was away in Jordan trying to persuade King Hussein's government that her work among Palestinian women under occupation in the West Bank needed greater help urgently. A large number of impoverished women depended upon Fareidah's initiative for their livelihood. On the face of it, she ran a first class example of an income-generating scheme. It was self-help in effective action. The women used their traditional needlecraft skills to make stoles and vestments for churches in Jerusalem and for visitors from around the world. The shop was filled with the beautiful and highly skilled handiwork of the Palestinian women. But Fareidah faced the problems of the Occupation which were mountainous and there was an air of desolation and despair about the place. The stocks were piling up and the number of tourists was falling. She had to buy cloth and pay the Israelis an ever-increasing rate of tax for it, in order to keep the women working. Then she had to pay the women for their work and they, in turn, also suffered ever-increasing Israeli taxation so that both the employer and the employee were working harder but receiving less. Now to complete the sorry story the Israelis were producing, by machine, stoles and vestments of her design and style which could be sold more cheaply. Fareidah had a big heart but no business brain. If only her designs had been patented, but she had never heard of such things as patents. So she was suffering the squeeze of double taxation, without the sales. It was a path to ruin and it would take a great many hard-working women and their families to ruin with her. It was a sad story, oft repeated among Palestinians trying to help themselves. My puny gift was no more than a goodwill gesture and a reminder of friendship, when she returned.

It seemed a good idea to head for another old friend, Mohammed the Camel Man, at the top of the Mount of Olives. A short cut across the goat tracks and through the olive groves would lead to the "Peace Garden" and a pleasant pause on the climb to the top. That plan didn't work either. The heat got to me and on the steep and stony part the sweat sprang out of me, though it dried instantly, leaving a salt taste round my mouth and a sting in the eyes. A rest was called for. There was a cave nearby which was rather smelly, but it would give shade. As I was bending to enter it, a dog dashed out with a bark that sent me back a pace or two. It was a pathetic flea-bitten creature and was probably barking from fear so I went back to the cave for the shade. It was so shaded that it took a while for the eyes to register. Then I saw it. A man's face, pale as paper, staring straight at me, but with unseeing eyes. I came out, twice as fast as I had gone in. For sure, the man was dead. The skinny scabby dog, tail between its legs, was cowering under a scrubby shrub. My skin, no longer burning hot, was one great goose pimple and my spine seemed to have turned to an icicle. My first thought was to run up to the top of the Mount of Olives and tell Mohammed but he knew me well and when the Police came the questioning and the reports might go on for the length of my journey. Not a good idea. The obvious thing was to walk back the way I had come, looking all calm, disappear into the milling crowds of the Old City and never say anything to anybody. But first, another quick look. It was all true. He was propped on an old mattress. Flies were coming out of his nose. Suddenly it seemed right to go to the nearby 'Casa' where the owners of the field lived. My name was not known to them and there would be no need to give it.

At the Casa a very fat woman (*all* Greek Orthodox women seem to take pride in a healthy size) answered the door. For some unaccountable reason, I tried to communicate in French, repeating "morte" several times and pointing toward the dog and the cave, both just in view. She showed so little surprise that I couldn't be sure she understood. She said 'OK' quite a lot and my French was just sufficient to understand that her husband was due home 'in a minute'. I made a few more gestures about stretchers and finally, with as much dramatic effect as possible, drew my hand across my throat, closing my eyes and gasping at the same time. With that I made my exit, stage right in haste, to continue my nice quiet day.

At the top of the Mount of Olives Mohammed greeted me with the customary kisses and welcomed the 300 Marlborough I was still carrying. It seemed wise not to mention the body down the hill and to listen instead to his ceaseless flow about God and the condition of the world. He laughed his old toothless laugh about Americans. "They have no brain. Only big pocket they have. They are so stupid. But money does not buy brains. Just watch, my brother. One day God will put them right. Then their heads will go down and their legs will be up. Yes, my brother, it will be a great crash. God wills it."

Mohammed, as ever, was the embodiment of traditional Moslem fatalism. What God wanted would happen, regardless of what we might think or do about it. So we might as well do nothing. No work, planning, building, developing was worthwhile. In fact, it was all quite foolish, if not immoral. In the face of such old fundamentalism, it was easy to see why the Arabs were divided among themselves. Traditionalists and progressives would never agree. Strangely, on the Israeli side there is the same divide.

While Mohammed and I were sitting and he was putting the world to rights on the steps of the Chapel of the Ascension, two armoured vehicles with a dozen police and soldiers arrived and screeched to a halt. With a lot of shouting, they all started running down the hillside, except one who stayed with the vehicles and lit a cigarette. After a while, he strolled over and sat with us. Mohammed asked him what the trouble was. The soldier said a man was dead and immediately asked Mohammed where he had got his 300 Marlborough. "My brother," he said, pointing to me, and the Israeli with the gun began questioning me about the cost, and how long I had known Mohammed. At that point, Mohammed decided it was time to pray and he disappeared into the Mosque, taking his cigarettes with him, and I decided it was time to melt into the crowds of the Old City and recognised that 'Quiet Days' have never been too common in Jerusalem.

Friday, 5th September 1986

Breakfast at St. George's Cathedral hostel is always interesting. There's no telling who the latest visitors will be. Today the fellow who sat next to me was employed by an American charity based in Cyprus. He spent three weeks in each month travelling in the Occupied Territories of Gaza and the West Bank, advising on the use of funds in Social and Relief Work among Palestinian refugees. He used St. George's as a base and spent the fourth week each month in his Cyprus office, from which he administered the charity and received visitors from Lebanon, Syria, Jordan and other Arab countries. He was free until mid-day, so we walked up the Mount of Olives and, sitting in the 'Pope's Garden' set apart for quiet reflection and prayers for peace, he told his story.

He described the great wealth of many Arabs and the hopeless poverty of others. He marvelled that such extremes seemed to be accepted as a fact of life. He described the ever greater hardships imposed by ever increasing Israeli taxation which was crippling the hardest working and most productive Palestinians, a taxation made necessary to pay for the Israeli war against Palestinians in the Lebanon. Again, he wondered how the Palestinians could live with the thought that they were financing the war against their own kith and kin. He described the difficulties he faced in ensuring that the funds he distributed actually reached the people for whom they were intended. Those who should receive the benefits were too power-less, too illiterate and too inarticulate to fend for themselves. "How can the blind see what is happening? How can the handicapped make their claims? How can those imprisoned without trial make themselves heard?" His sad conclusion was that the Middle East was not a compassionate area, that only those as hard as nails survived. "The weak do go to the wall, the fittest do survive," he said.

His gravest concern was over education, or the lack of it. "At every opportunity the Israelis close the Universities," he said. "They do not want educated Palestinians. Fewer and fewer children go to school. An ignorant and idle generation is growing up. That will be trouble." It is obvious to him, and to me, that the uneducated will be fodder for the Islamic fundamentalists. They will be the ones who rebel and make jihad. What Israel needs is intelligent, educated, progressive neighbours. Out of fear they are creating the opposite which will be even more fearful. And they can't see it.

It was evident he was a troubled person and his story was a sad one. "Yet," he concluded, "it has always been so in this land. The people expect no other and an indomitable spirit of high hopes and good cheer remains, without any apparent justification." At noon, he returned to the City. He had the job which I would most like, though whether I would have the courage and the calm to face its frustrations was another matter.. In fact, when I told him how much I admired his work and would like his job, he said "It would break your heart."

Tuesday, 29th September 1987

American Evangelism

In the afternoon, I went to the Mount of Olives and to the 'Pope's Garden', confident that I would enjoy the peace and quiet which had been missing in the morning visit to the Church of the Holy Sepulchre.

I should have known better! A foolish hope! After climbing all that way, in very great heat, it was disappointing to find a television crew installed and a religious film in the making. I was signalled away, but climbed up higher to give myself a better view. The film was American, of course. And the broadcaster was declaiming about The Second Coming of Christ which was due on the Mount of Olives and was imminent. All his Biblical quotes (and there were dozens) were from Paul or Revelation. The film was declaring that the Second Coming was dependent on two Scriptural requirements being fulfilled. The first was that the Anti-Christ who had to be defeated should come among us. That was the Pope. The second was that God's Chosen People should return to the land He have given them. That was the Israeli occupation. So both requirements had been met. Scripture had been fulfilled and the Second Coming was about to happen, and from that very spot on the Mount of Olives. "That is what Christianity is all about," he drawled. This was a classic example of the devil citing Scripture for his own purpose, and further proof that the Bible can be used to prove anything you may want to prove. I felt their presence and the film was an absolute abuse of the Garden which was given, as an ecumenical gesture, to pray for unity. This was the reverse. It was offensive.

What is it about Jerusalem that sends people so crazy? And with all these fanatics, Moslem, Jewish and Christian, will it ever know peace? No wonder Jesus wept over Jerusalem, and his tears must have been shed from a spot very close to where this dreadful film is being made.

Wednesday, 30th September 1987

Undignified Retreat

My fascination with the Mount of Olives and the 'Peace Garden' continues. There is never a visit which does not provide something of interest.

This time it was two little girls of no more than five or six years who destroyed my hopes of peace and quiet. They came and stared, the way Arab children do, getting nearer and nearer until they finally asked for "Baksheesh" in between giggles. One girl had lost nearly all her hair and the bald patches had spots of congealed blood. I didn't know what the disease might be but she looked disgusting. The other had a runny nose which made an even more repulsive sight. There is obviously a shortage of tissues in this land. So they looked a grimy, grisly pair and, when they got too close, I said "Goodbye" in my most assertive way and pushed the little monsters away. I was immediately ashamed and imagined Our Lord who would probably have cuddled them (ugh!) but I had made a tactical mistake and I was as good as beaten. They settled just beyond reach, but near enough to throw stones and taunt me with an excellent mimicry of "Goodbye". So, after half a dozen stones and a few spits had found their target, I left the Pope's Holy Garden of Prayer, feeling a little like the United States leaving Vietnam or the Russians not knowing how to withdraw from Afghanistan. I comforted myself by picturing it as a symbol of the victory little Palestine may one day win over mighty Israel – by obstinately staying there, and being mildly awkward.

Wednesday, 7th October 1987

Ecumenism or Exclusion?

Today it was third time lucky in the 'Pope's Garden', the place of prayer for Unity, on the Mount of Olives. Remembering the vile and aggressive evangelical Americans who had been making their wretched TV film and the two pathetic little girls who did a 'Vietnam' on me, there was no telling what would happen this time. In fact, the experience which awaited was a mix of the lovely and the awful, as is so often the case in this beautiful plagued land. A French pilgrim party arrived to celebrate Mass.

They were elderly and over-laden, rather typical pilgrims. They sang the Mass cheerfully and the Taizé choruses made it possible for me to join in, which they seemed to appreciate. In fact, at 'The Peace' the kisses welcomed me heartily. And then came the Communion and the Priest, host in hand, approached me. "Catholic?" he enquired. "English," I replied. "Anglican." "Ah, non! non! Impossible!" said he, and passed me by. Yet this was the Ecumenical Garden, the place founded by Pope and Protestant as the place of Unity. It was such a shame. They seemed to be such lovely people. If they had had their way they would have welcomed me. But the system does not allow it. What do Catholics gain from this exclusion? It makes them seem so arrogant, so rude, so inhospitable. Imagine having friends at home and feeding some, but not the others. It was a puzzle, and a painful one.

When they had left the Garden and peace was restored, I continued reading Karen Armstrong's book "The Break with Jerusalem". It tells the story of Paul's conflict with the Jerusalem church and the first words that came to sight expressed exactly the sad experience just suffered: *"Christians who seek to impose identity of belief on each other have lost their sense of God's greatness."* She goes on to recognise that all sects have done it. … *"Unless you believe what I believe, you are damned… is to limit God, to the capacity of human institution."* That is what the French Catholics had just done to me.

"Christians who believe exactly what they are told to believe," she concluded, *"may feel secure but not only have they abandoned their intellectual responsibility,*

they have also cut God down to the size of their system." This was food and drink to me. *"God is always bigger than any one man's vision, even if that one man be named Paul."* It was good to read these things on the Mount of Olives, where the whole story was brought to birth in the first place.

Thursday, 8th October 1987

Anglican Genius

The weather was changing, clouds appeared with a cool breeze. The 'early rains' could be on their way. For the first time the Holy City viewed from the Pope's Garden was more grey than gold. Suddenly a young man came into the Garden looking very much under a cloud. He approached me and asked quite forcefully "Do you know much about this place?" It turned out he was angry because he had just enrolled at the Hebrew University nearby only to be told he had to find his own tutor and his own accommodation.

Dirk, aged 28, was a lecturer in theology at Ghent University and had won an Israeli scholarship to study "Judaic tradition and archaeology". He was fluent in twelve languages – Dutch (his own) and what he called the 'home' languages Flemish, French and German; the 'Biblical' languages Hebrew, Greek, Latin and the ancient Chaldean; the languages of the Levant, Arabic, modern Hebrew and Yiddish together with English. I was impressed. But he was angry. After winning a scholarship he did not expect to have to find his own accommodation and he had no idea how to set about it. The University had refused to allow him to leave his luggage and the police had put it under surveillance until he had an address. I calmed him down with the promise of an introduction to the Anglican hostel at the Cathedral. The discovery that I was an Anglican opened the theological floodgates.

Dirk announced that if he were not a Dutch Reformed theologian "by birth" he would be an Anglican "by choice". "You Anglicans have a genius," he announced, to my surprise. "You allow people to think, you allow them a conscience, you allow them to grow and be themselves". It was a nice change to have our Church of England praised. "You are unique," he said. "The Catholics, the Orthodox and the old Calvinists all forced people to think and believe alike. They wanted robots, not humans," he declared. He then explained that 'old Calvinism' was dead, at least in his academic circles, and that he belonged to a reformed Calvinism with "less doctrine and more action". By then he had forgotten his frustration and was enjoying his

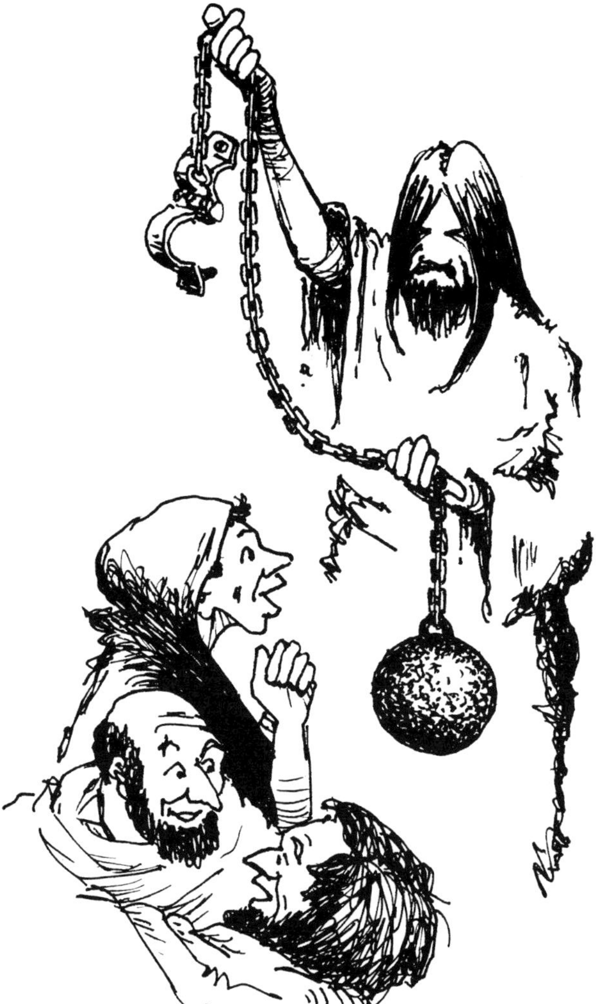

theology. "The whole Bible," he said, "is stories. Except Paul, who introduces Theology – doctrine." Dirk traced the stories from the opening of Genesis (the Creation story) – to the end of Revelation – (visions and dreams). The Gospels were stories. And the central character of the Gospels was the story teller par excellence. The Book of Acts was the story of the Early Church, as the Old Testament was the story of the Hebrew or Jewish people. The whole Middle East tradition, both Jewish and Moslem was built upon story telling. They never built a theology. To this day, they do not say "You must believe this…" They only say "You must *do* this." And Jesus was within that tradition. "Go and *do* likewise", hence the two Great Commandments: love your God, etc., etc. and your neighbour as yourself; eventually summarised into "A new Commandment I give you – love one another." A Doing. Not a Doctrine.

"Then came Paul, who never knew Jesus, from a different (Greek) tradition, wanting to spread the message to the Gentile world. But what message? That caused the most bitter clash with the Jewish Christians in Jerusalem – Peter, James and John particularly – and Paul went his own way to spread his fervent faith across Asia Minor and the known world. But it was his interpretation of the faith. And he left out the story and built the theological edifice that has led to creeds, dogmas, heresy-hunts, divisions: it has turned Christianity from the simplicity of 'doing' to the complexity of 'Doctrine' – and true doctrine, OR ELSE! The Judgement will not be based on correct belief," Dirk concluded. "That is too cerebral. It shackles where it should liberate."

I was absorbed, and he must have been too, because he had to be reminded about St. George's, his luggage and the tutor he still had to find. We left the Garden, walked down hill and at Gethsemene took a taxi to the hostel. He booked in at St. Georges and I hoped his time living with Anglicans wouldn't spoil his notion of our genius.

Anyway, he has agreed to walk with me to Desert monasteries, as soon as he has a tutor.

Wednesday, 23rd January 2002

Five Years Later . . . Palestine Paralysed

The last day of my journey came as a great relief. There was the strong feeling that one tragedy would continue to follow the other with monotonous and depressing repetition. I had been in the country eight days. In that time the Israelis had entered Ramallah where they had put Arafat under house arrest and had blown up his media headquarters. This was in retaliation for a suicide terrorist's act in which six Israelis had been murdered at a family barmitzvah party. That attack was itself revenge for the Israeli assassination of a Palestinian military leader who had been responsible for an attack on an Israeli bus station, which was in response to the Israelis who had bulldozed 53 Palestinian homes, leaving 400 homeless in Rafa. All this in a week. The Israelis were insisting Arafat must control his people. Quite right. But how can he when they have closed his Jerusalem HQ, bombed his Gaza base, blown up his helicopters, dug up his airstrips, burnt down his police offices, shot down his advisers and put him under house arrest? I had not met anyone who had seen a way out of the political impasse, a light at the end of the tunnel. "After all," said one, "it began with Isaac and Ishmael, the rival sons of Abraham, and it's got steadily worse ever since, so why should it stop now?"

However, today one thing was different. The sun, which had been hidden all week, was shining from a brilliantly blue sky. A walk to the top of the Mount of Olives seemed a good idea so I skirted the Old City walls, walked past Gethsemene and began the long climb slowly. There wasn't a soul in sight. Even Gethsemene, where a dozen hawkers, several taxi drivers and a couple of camel owners are usually seeking business, was deserted. Half way up I reached the 'Peace Garden' and the chance to take a breather, enjoy the panoramic view over the Old City and pray for peace, which is the purpose of the place. The great gates were padlocked. That annoyed me. There was no reason to lock out prayers so I scaled the stone wall which had a number of convenient footholds and dropped down on the garden side. I wondered if some security network had spotted me and whether someone might assume I was up to no good, about to fire a rocket across the Kidron

Valley and on to the Dome of the Rock. But no alarms sounded so I viewed the old memorials to Pope Paul VI and Marc Boegner, who founded the place, and the new memorial to the late Archbishop George Appleton who had dedicated it, fifteen years earlier, when peace had seemed a possibility. I looked at the Golden City, bathed in sunlight and marvelled that such a tiny place looking so benign and so beautiful could be the fount of such volcanic fury, century after century, age upon age. Surely, if the world breaks into a third conflagration the injustices of this place will be the cause. My prayer was added to all the others that flowed from that place but I had the feeling that prayers for peace had about as much effect as Canute trying to turn back the tide.

No one was in sight. It was not until I had climbed over the garden wall and through the olive grove on the way to the top of the Mount that someone at last came into sight. It was a small boy and his goat. It was quite a relief to see somebody.

Monday, 3rd June 2003

The long hot climb up the Mount of Olives to the "Peace Garden" was all too predictably silent and lonely.

At Gethsemene, usually busy with hawkers and pilgrims, not a soul was in sight. The 'Enter' and 'Exit' signs at the church declared the place to be open but the only person at the gate had found a shady spot and was fast asleep. If any evidence that business is bad was needed, that was surely it.

At the Peace Garden, the gate was open but there was no one inside and the pipes, which used to jet some water, were inactive so that it took some while to cool down in the shade of an olive tree. The view of the Old City and its holy places was as spellbinding as ever but, with no visitors at all and no conversations to stimulate the mind, it was champagne without the bubbles.

The second part of the climb to the top, across the stony olive groves, was as exhausting as the first part, so a cup of tea in the luxury of the Seven Arches Hotel seemed a good idea. It was Arab Jerusalem's star hotel, which isn't surprising because its original purpose was to be King Hussein's winter palace and it was built to suit the style of an Arab King. From the 7 Arches at the front, he would have overlooked the whole of the Holy City and from the 7 Arches at the back he would have looked across the wilderness to the Jordan River, with Jericho's oasis in the left distance, the Dead Sea in front and the Herodian in the right distance. In short, he would have been able to keep an eye on his Western Kingdom. Unfortunately, he never lived in it as the Israeli victory in the 1967 seven-day war left him with no Kingdom west of the Jordan to look over. The palace-that-never-was became the luxury hotel-that-is and a good place for a cup of tea. But it wasn't. The lawns, once manicured to perfection, were uncut. The roses were being throttled by weeds, though some still bloomed weakly. Inside, the great hall and spacious galleries were empty and footsteps echoed, as if in a morgue. At 'Reception' the immaculately uniformed attendant was asleep. It seemed unkind to disturb him. Then came the dining suite, once magnificently laid with crystal and silver but now without the prospect of any diners. And if there had been any diners, they would not have seen the panoramic view of the old Kingdom because the huge picture windows were thickly coated with the desert dust of the winter sandstorms. Clearly, all the staff had been laid off and this was not the place even for a cup of tea.

Chapter Two

The Wilderness

THE MONASTERY OF TEMPATIONS

May 1984

Purging Memories

Bad memories of Jericho haunted me. It was the result of a nightmare experience on my first visit, in 1981.

I had been part of a pilgrim party suffering, as most pilgrims do, from an overcrowded programme. On that awful day, in the high heat of August, we had been taken to the top of Mount Masada, we had bathed in the Dead Sea (lowest point on the earth's surface, and probably the hottest) and then we had traipsed round the sun-soaked ruins of Qumran, the site associated with the Dead Sea Scrolls. That was more than enough for most of us – but no, we were then driven to Jericho and dragooned to the top of the famous 'tell' to hear of the fifteen (or was it thirty?) civilisations which made Jericho the oldest inhabited place on earth. And the hottest. Why, oh why do pilgrimage companies overcrowd the programme? It's a miracle that more pilgrims do not die in the chase. How often pilgrim parties can be seen staggering around, looking culture-shocked, heat-exhausted and more dead than alive!

And that is how it was on that awful day. Then we had been taken to the '7 Trees' restaurant for lunch. Lunch! In that heat! Water and a fresh orange or one of the pineapples from Jericho's plentiful oasis, yes, but hot lunch, no. I had left the table and stretched out in the garden under the shade of another table, exhausted. Completely. And within a moment, two salesmen hawking bracelets or necklaces or something, had knelt beside me. 'We offer special price ... velly nice stone ... make your lady happy ....' Couldn't they see that I was about to expire and a necklace for my lady was not my top priority at that moment? It was a dreadful day and Jericho was a dreadful place. When we eventually got into the air conditioned coach, the guide drew our attention to a monastery high in the mountains. "The Mount of Temptations," he said, "where Jesus was 40 days and 40 nights in the Wilderness." It looked a wild and craggy place. "How does anyone get there?"

I asked. "God knows," the guide said, and the coach started the long climb back to Jerusalem.

At that moment it never occurred to me that I would set foot in the dreaded Jericho ever again, much less that I would ever climb to that monastery, hidden in the hills.

Three years had passed, and the way to purge the bad memory was to climb up to the monastery and find out how to get there. So, at the same 7 Trees restaurant it was time to order fresh orange, drink it at the very same table which had once sheltered me, and set my face to the Mount of Temptations.

Jericho's tarmac roads were burning hot and there was a haze of dust and heat which half obscured the monastery but, once clear of the town, there were banana plantations, olive groves, a mountain spring and the clear sight of a snake path winding up to the monastery. A donkey laden with supplies was on the trail.

The track was fully exposed to the sun. Standing still was worse than moving. Movement created a little air current which came as a relief. The other relief was the spectacular view coming into sight with every burning step. The oasis of Jericho below, the Jordan river beyond, like a sliver of silver, and the mountains of Moab, from which Moses had first seen the Promised Land 'flowing with milk and honey', in the background. At the monastery door, the achievement of the long climb filled me with pride and I looked down on the world as if master of all I surveyed. That, of course, was two of the temptations.

The massive monastery door had a notice :

No women
No guns
No shorts

I rang, and after a long wait the door creaked open and a youth said "Do you have gun?" I said "No, but I want water." Inside, the stone walls gave shade, the flagstone floor was cool and water was brought. The youth seemed nervous, and to every question he answered "The father is resting, he sleep." "No, you can't see any further. Privat! Privat!" It wasn't a disappointment. I had arrived, satisfied my curiosity, laid the evil ghost of 1981 and was too exhausted to want to go any further. At the door, the youth told me his name was Marwan. "I am Christian from Ramallah," he said. And when he showed me out he said "Very bad men in mountains. God go with you."

Back at the 7 Trees for another fresh orange juice, the waiter did not believe I had walked to the monastery. "No, not possible," he said. "Only strong men and donkeys do that." On the bus back to Jerusalem a Swedish youth lent me a Travellers Guide and it had a sentence about the monastery *"now largely derelict, entry is difficult and hospitality nil. The best thing about it is the door at the back which provides access to the mountain top."* I hadn't known about that.

Next time ... next time ... if I ever climb up there again.

Thursday, 9th May 1985

Marwan and the American

The memory of the monastery in the mountains at Jericho fascinated me. I knew how hard a climb it was to reach it and that there was no other access. How could medical help ever reach the monks? How did an old or frail monk ever get down? Perhaps they didn't. Perhaps the place was full of ancient monks, trapped for ever. Where could they be buried, on that solid rock face? How was water stored in that barren wilderness? And anyway, when had it last rained in Jericho? All these puzzles drew me back to the mountain to the very place where Jesus spent his forty days and nights. My intention was to climb up and get in, to ask to be let out of the door at the back and to see where the path led. So an early start, 7.00 am from the Arab bus station, and in under the hour, it was time to begin the long climb.

It was the same young man, Marwan, who opened the door and he recognised me from twelve months ago. It was flattering to be recognised in such a remote spot, until he said that he seldom had more than one visitor in a week, sometimes only one in a month, so he remembered them all.

He agreed to let me out of the back door to climb to the top but he told me the door was always bolted because of "bad men in the mountains" and that an agreed knock was necessary for my return and that it should be at exactly 2.00 p.m. So we synchronised watches.

It was the hell of a climb to the top; steep, stony, barren and sun-soaked. No wonder Jesus was "an hungered" after 40 days and nights up there. No wonder he imagined devils and saw visions. And it would seem as if the whole world was at his feet.

From the top it was possible to see the distant spires of Jerusalem behind, on the Western skyline; to the South the steely strip of the Dead Sea glinted; to the North, the Jordan Valley wound its way toward Galilee; below, at the foot of the mountain, the ancient City of Jericho huddled midst its oasis of fruit trees; straight ahead rose the mountains of the Moabites, now called Jordan, from which Moses first gave the command for Joshua and his army to cross the River and claim the Promised Land. And all around were the shacks of those who had become refugees in the struggles which had robbed Palestinians of their homes in modern times. Jesus certainly climbed to a significant spot when he first went into the Wilderness to review his situation, and his nation's.

I was quietly admiring the scene and thinking these thoughts when a stranger arrived, carrying a gun, as many Israelis tend to do. "Where in the world are you going?" he asked. It was easy to tell that he was an American. "To the monastery door," I replied, and immediately he wanted to come with me. "You will not be allowed in because you are carrying a gun," I told him. Everyone knew the monastery rule about guns, a rule which applied for all religious buildings throughout the Holy Land, but he still came on with me. It was a steep descent. He would regret it when he had to retrace those steps uphill in the heat of the day. At the monastery door, I gave the special knock. "Tell him I am your buddy," said the American with the gun. Marwan held the great door ajar, only his nose and eyes showing. "No guns," he said to the American. "How the hell am I to get back to Jericho then?" he shouted at the doorkeeper, who repeated "No guns." The American put his foot in the doorway. "Who's gonna stop me?" he said, wedging the door open. It was obvious he and I would be barred and the long uphill climb with a bad tempered armed Israeli held no appeal, so I stepped into the doorway and said "No guns. You know the law. I told you. He told you. No guns." The next moment I was in the monastery, sitting on the stone floor, and Marwan was slamming the great bolts, shut. "You like tea?" he said as he helped me off the floor. "Sorry I hurt you but I have to move quick." There was a noise like a firecracker and a thud in the bolted door. "You see why I move quick!" he said. The American had put a bullet in the door.

Inside the monastery, we drank tea, black with sugar, while sitting on a stone seat in a dark corridor. "You are my brother," he said, gratefully recognising my help. "Last year, three men with guns went into a monastery and stole all the ikons." So it was that he told his story. He was a Christian of the Greek Orthodox church, born and educated in the Palestinian township of Ramallah, now Occupied Territory on the West Bank. He had won University entrance but, owing to all the problems attached to Higher Education in the Occupied Territories, he had accepted the offer of a place at Leningrad University, to read Economics. There he had spent the first year mastering the Russian language and the following four years studying in Russian and passing the exams in Russian. He showed me his degree certificate, sealed with wax and framed behind glass, the only treasure in an otherwise bare stone cell. I marvelled at the effort required to learn such a strange language, at the deprivation he must have suffered in those Russian winters so far from home, and at the determination he must have had to stick it for five years. "The sad thing is," he concluded, "it is all a waste." And he explained that he had absolutely no chance of employment. "The Israelis provide their own economists, mostly from America," he said. "What Jew would employ a Russian-trained Arab?" The problem was evident. "So I am the doorman at the monastery." I asked if he was happy there. "It is not possible to be happy in an Occupied Land," he replied. "I should be in Ramallah with my people. I should be married. I should be an economist or an accountant, with a father's pride in his family. I should not be the doorman, hiding in a mountain monastery." I sat quietly, grateful for the dates and the fresh water that he had brought. "If I go back to Ramallah," he mused, "the first time there is trouble and shooting the Army will take me away. They always take the educated. They do not like us to be educated. So I stay here. It is all I can do."

He showed me out of the monastery by the front door after he had checked through a spy hole that there was no one with a gun outside. "You are all right. The American will still be climbing the other way," he said, and we parted, sad yet laughing.

The questions with which the day began had not been answered. And now there were a whole lot of new questions to puzzle me. One thing was certain. Marwan's wilderness would last more than 40 days and 40 nights.

Monday, 16th March 1987

Crying in the Wilderness

It was dark. And very cold. We were waiting at the border for passport clearance. We had been waiting some time. "It is easier to cross from East to West Berlin than to cross this border," said a disgruntled German. The border was between Egypt and Israel, in the disputed region of Taba. There were four small huts with corrugated iron roofs and, apart from that –nothing. A hundred yards to the East, the Red Sea. A hundred yards to the West, wild and barren mountains. To the South, the long flat desert wastes. Nothing except those four huts. One sign said 'Bureau de Change' but it was locked up. Another said 'Customs' but the only official was watching television. The delay was at the hut marked 'Passports'. We had been there two hours. Just waiting. Occasionally an official strolled out and we thought something might happen. But he always strolled back again, and nothing did happen. "It's no use hurrying them," said our driver. "They like this moment of power." A scraggy dog crossed the road, almost the only sign of life. And it was so cold. The wind hurtled round the huts, the corrugated iron rattled and the sand blew in our faces. I wondered why I ever got involved in travel, and especially at these Israeli borders. A name was called. One of the Germans went into the hut. "This will take an age," said my companion. "They give Germans a tough time." So we waited. And we waited. In 'No man's land'. Then came a sound – the only sound, save the wind and the sea. It came from behind us, from Egypt. A lone voice. A Moslem intoning the call to prayer, at nightfall. We peered into the gloom… There he was, a solitary figure behind the barbed wire of the border, facing Mecca, bowing to the ground and chanting his lonesome prayer. A voice crying in the wilderness.

Next day (yes, we did get through in the end), I was in the Jordan Valley climbing to the Monastery of the Temptations, high in the mountains above Jericho. For a thousand years it had been a place of monastic silence and seclusion. A thousand monks used to inhabit the mountain caves of the region and every year a thousand pilgrims came to pray. Now, there was sophisticated radar equipment on the mountain top, and Israeli military bases all around. Israeli music blared out of the camps. A thousand soldiers had destroyed the silence and seclusion of the centuries. I knocked on the monastery door. After a while, the spy hole cover flicked back and a voice said "Have you gun?" I said I had come to pray. The great door creaked open and let me in, then it was shut behind me, bolted and barred. The monk was apologetic. He brought water and some cake, but it was the Great Lenten fast, so he wouldn't have any himself. I wanted to ask what had happened to Marwan, but the monk's English was limited and it didn't seem appropriate. He took me to the ancient Chapel to light a candle and offer prayers. When I left, he thanked me for prayers, signed me with the sign of the cross and said he must return to the Chapel, because he was now the only monk remaining. No longer a thousand monks, but just one, surrounded by all that hostile military power. So I went my way, and he returned to his solitary life. Another voice, crying in the wilderness.

These lone voices – the Moslem facing Mecca and the monk in the mountains, do they achieve anything? What is it that drives them on, alone and against the elements? Is it all useless? Will these last remnants soon be blotted out and will military might rule unhindered? It seemed inevitable. And yet… and yet… it was in this same Wilderness that Elijah took refuge in a mountain cave (now the monastery of St. George) and it was there that he cried out to the Lord *"I, only I, am left and they seek my life to take it away."* And it was from this same Wilderness that John the Baptist came, a lone voice, crying in the wilderness that the rough places be made smooth (now commemorated at the Monastery of Deir Hajlah). And it was on this very mountain that Jesus fasted forty days and forty nights struggling with temptations and shaping his ministry, all alone. So there was plenty of precedent for the solitary life, in fact the lonely monk at the Monastery of the Temptations caught the spirit of the wilderness. It would have been good to say all these things to the isolated monk, but the limitations of language prevented it.

None the less there is hope in this wilderness, in the midst of military bases, armed forces and radar reconnaissance, there is hope for the remnant in these desert places, now, as there always has been.

25th November 1999

High Hopes or False Dawn?

I couldn't believe my eyes. I was in the middle of Jericho, and what did I see? To my amazement there was a Cable Car rising from the heart of Jericho and travelling up into the Mount of Temptations and there, alongside the ancient monastery was a modern restaurant. It could have been a European ski resort, and dozens of tourists were buying tickets for the tour, so I joined them.

Sure enough, the cabin sky-lifted us over the very paths and tracks I had often trodden so painfully in blazing summer sun, and within five minutes we were emptied out onto a platform alongside the air-conditioned restaurant, in sight of the monastery. There were dozens of us. Some went for a drink, others to see the view through telescopes, and a goodly number went up the steps to the monastery, myself among them.

The great door was open, the "no guns, no women, no shorts" notice was gone, and several women were entering. A monk was welcoming tourists and speaking good English. "Here we have eight monks," he was saying. "We pray the Liturgy and we welcome visitors. This is our life." What had happened to Marwan who had opened the door to a visitor once a week "sometimes once a month." What had happened to the monk who had said he was there alone. What had happened?

Politically, Jericho was no longer under Israeli control. The Palestinian Authority, which is the proposed Palestinian State in embryonic form, governed Jericho. It had received substantial funds from the European Union and it was developing Tourism so that it could generate its own funding. The cable car into the Mount of Temptations was its showpiece. And a very spectacular showpiece it was. That is what had happened.

This place has always posed questions and it still does, but not as before. Previously the puzzle was about monastic life, now it is a question of international politics. If the Israelis refuse to allow a Palestinian State, what will happen to all this investment? If the Israelis renege on the Oslo Peace Plan, will there be any tourists?

Two things are certain – one is that the Cable Car is a startling indication of what could be achieved in a Palestinian State. The other is that the Monastery of the Temptations is now facing more temptations than it ever could have dreamed of.

Monday, 21st January 2002

No Go in Jericho

There was very little to do, and it was bitterly cold. In normal circumstances, it would be good to go to Jericho which, as the lowest inhabited spot on earth, is always a lot warmer than lofty windswept Jerusalem. But with one voice advisers said "Don't go." The road blocks were many, the security intense, the people demoralised and there was nothing there anyway. Some said it had become an enclave for Arab hard-liners and anyone who entered was immediately recorded by security and suspect from then on. No Israeli entered or passed through Jericho any more. A new road had been built which was for Israeli cars so that they could travel unhindered.

In one way this was a new development but in another way it was as old as the hills. In Jesus' time there had been trouble for travellers in Jericho. Those who went up for the Festival from Galilee to Jerusalem through Jericho invariably feared bandits or the rogues who provided protection at a price, of whom Zaccheus has become the prototype. So those old-time travellers had sought another route, a way of skirting Jericho. Today's Jews were doing the same. They could go to the Israeli bus station, catch an Israeli bus to Galilee and travel on the new road all the way, by-passing Jericho, and arriving at Tiberias on the lakeside in one hour. But that had no appeal to me. It was the old city of Jericho, the oasis in the wilderness, that appealed to me. It was the climb up to the monastery in the mountain and the old track to Jerusalem through the mountains that drew me to Jericho, again and again. It was the idea of all those pilgrims down the ages, including Jesus, trailing through the wilderness that fired my imagination. The idea of an Israeli coach, with all mod cons, speeding along new tarmac held no appeal at all.

But at this Jerusalem hotel, what could I do? I was the only guest in the 200 rooms. 80 members of staff had been laid off and the only one remaining spoke no English and shuffled around in a raincoat. There was no heating, erratic electricity and no food provided. Yet in the past we had enjoyed high hospitality there, and warm friendship with staff and pilgrims. What could I do all day? Walk in the empty suk and see the shops, all shuttered? Not much fun. I was trapped. In a cold dark building. This is what the Palestinians face, day after day. I would be released from my trap, in another few days, I would be home. For them, they would remain caught in the cage of their living prison. Is it any wonder the young ones rebel? I would.

Friday, 6th June 2003

For years, Jericho has provided a traveller's challenge. One challenge is the heat. The lowest inhabited spot on the earth is often the hottest spot on the earth, where the heat sears off the desert and burns everything in its path. A second challenge is the climb into the mountains to the Monastery of the Temptations, a steep and rugged pathway if ever there was one. Another challenge is finding the 'Old' or 'New Testament' Jericho, now an archaeological site some way removed from present-day Jericho. But the challenges are rewarding. The sight of the cleft between the mountains through which Jesus and all the pilgrims of ancient times would have made their way up to Jerusalem is breathtaking. It requires no imagination to see the dangers confronting every pilgrim party. Suddenly the story of the man who fell among thieves on the way from Jerusalem to Jericho reveals another of the challenges travellers face. And the mountains are pock-marked with caves, making it easy to imagine the hermit monks who dwelt there in Byzantine times and equally easy to imagine the brigands who replaced them in later times and terrorised every traveller. In short, Jericho is absolutely unique and its challenges have been unlimited, in every age. Not least for Joshua when he crossed the Jordan and claimed the land for the Israelites, greatly helped by Rahab the prostitute who liked his soldiers and gave the vital signal; and then there was General Allenby, crossing at the same point and beginning the campaign that would end the Ottoman Empire and establish the British Mandate which was meant to restore the land to the Palestinians but ended by handing it to Jewry. Oh Jericho! Jericho! The intrigues and the challenges which echo around this little oasis where oranges, bananas and the finest fruits grow.

Today's challenges were of a different order. The challenge was to get there at all, and then get back. Some people said Jericho was closed and it would be a waste of effort. Certainly the people of Jericho are not allowed out. All that lovely fruit which they used to sell in Jerusalem and was their livelihood, would be going to waste. Other people said it was possible for foreigners to get in and out but only on foot, as no car could cross the checkpoints. It was a challenge that could not be refused.

In the event, it was possible to get there. But it took a lot of bloody-minded determination, the use of seven different vehicles, at the cost of 88 shekels (£15). It used to be possible to go on a Palestinian bus, direct, for 10p return. The cost was annoying but not prohibitive. In the context of travel, it was not exceptional. But for any local, even if they could get the necessary passes, it would be ruinous. This was the challenge:

First, find a 'service' vehicle to go to Abu Dis (the other side of Bethany). There exit. Goodbye to the first vehicle. Join the crowd at the checkpoint who are all in a bad mood, unsheltered from the sun and being pushed around by butts of guns, even women with babies. In fact the babies had to be removed from their mothers to show the bundle really was a baby. There were no female soldiers to do this investigation. The men protested, the women and the babies cried. When a soldier approaches and invites you to go straight through a channel headed "Foreigners", take it, even though you leave all the locals in a long cage.

Second, walk through 'No Man's Land'. After 200 metres, enter a second service vehicle to go to Jericho. Wait patiently until there are seven passengers.

If after half an hour there are still only three, refuse the driver's offer to go immediately if you pay for yourself and the missing four (fifty shekels instead of ten). Continue to wait, even if less patiently. Eventually, when you are seven, the journey will begin. At the Jericho checkpoint, get out. When all six others are turned back by Security soldiers, continue alone, painfully aware that you can travel in their homeland, and they can't.

Third, cross the long 'No Man's Land' on foot, hoping for another vehicle on the Jericho side. If none there, and no shade either, prepare for a long walk, on burning tarmac. When a fellow the other side of the road shouts out something in Arabic, reply "Good Morning"; unless you can think of anything better to say. When he offers a lift 'to the centre' take it, even at ten shekels, expensive for a ramshackle tub on wheels but it gets you there and does you both some good.

Fourth, walk through long empty streets, shops shuttered where there used to be banks of fresh oranges, pineapples and bananas, reach the cable car for the mountain monastery. It may not be working, but at least you will have arrived. It may have taken four hours, instead of the old twenty minutes. Finally, think of the locals, who can't do it at all.

Later in the day, the return journey had a similar pattern, with one worse feature. As locals could not get out of Jericho and I was the only person to pass the checkpoint and cross 'No Mans Land', I was the only one looking for a 'service vehicle'. Waiting for others would be like waiting for Godot, the chances of him coming ever more remote. Would I have to pay the full fare, about 70 shekels? After waiting what seemed an age under the shade of a tree, a big man arrived on a small donkey, which he tethered to a tree, and later a small man arrived on a big camel which was tethered to another tree. They were Bedouin, out of the wilderness, apparently exempt from checks, probably because in their nomadic life they manage to keep on the right side of road blocks and checkpoints. So we were three on the return to Jerusalem. Those were today's challenges.

The good part of the day was the climb to the Monastery which used to be a favourite challenge, some time ago. On my last two visits, the cable car had whisked me up into the mountain, in a flash. It was probable that my last climb on foot was ten years ago, or even before that. It is still steep, still rugged, but it was good to face the challenge of climbing again. The cable car's closure was a blessing, at least to me.

Inside the monastery, the monk, Hilarion, made it very clear that the closure of the cable car was a blessing to him, too. "The cable car was a foolish mistake," he said. "Who wants it? Only tourists, and there aren't any." And he explained that the Palestinian Authority now had to give free places to school groups and Moslem parties, to keep it going. Those groups, according to the monk, had no respect or understanding of the monastery which they invaded in large and disorderly numbers. "From September 1999, our life has been destroyed," he said. At one stage, they needed eight monks to cope with the crowds, but they had now reduced to two. He was obviously upset by the whole episode, so I hoped a light remark might help, but it didn't. My suggestion was that at least it was easier for the monks to come and go. "No," he said, "we never use it, we still walk." And the food and other necessities still came up by donkey. Eventually I asked his permission to leave by the back door and climb to the top of the mount. He was impressed that I knew about the back door, but he refused. "It is not possible," he said. "The tourist police forbid it." For some years, he explained, Palestinian militants had used the top of the mountain to fire into the Israeli army base at the top of the next mountain. The Israelis, as a result, were ready to fire at anyone on the mount, armed or unarmed. I was convinced and didn't press the point.

It was good to recall earlier visits, not least the time that an American with a gun had come down from the top with me and had shot the door when refused entry. On the way out, we looked down on Jericho, the oasis which Moses described as "the land flowing with milk and honey." It was still fruitful but there were huge uncultivated areas where once had been nursery gardens and crops in plenty. "They can not sell in Jerusalem," the monk said. "So they cultivate enough for themselves, that's all." The monk concluded "They live in a prison. They can go nowhere. And the economy of the West Bank is ruined. Jericho provided everything. And what does the Palestinian Authority do about it? It builds a cable car!"

THE MONASTERY IN THE WILDERNESS

Friday, 10th May 1985

Fasting in the Wilderness

Travelling alone is fun. No need for committee meetings to find the common mind, no need for consultations on whether to turn right or left, an ever-changing variety of companions along the way. But there is also a problem – there is supposed to be safety in numbers. Being alone can be dangerous and Joan, knowing this, had made me promise not to walk in the desert alone.

So it was necessary to look out for a likely companion for the desert trail to St. George's, the monastery in the wilderness, half-way to Jericho. And I found him in the Old City. It was dusk and the shutters were coming down and the alleys were already deserted. He was sitting outside a café, sipping water, and he looked lonely. "Do you speak English?" I asked. He did. So I sat down and went straight to the point – "Would you like to walk in the desert? I know the way from here to Jericho." He was excited by the idea, so we agreed to meet at the top of the Mount of Olives, in the morning at 5.00 a.m.

Back at the hostel, it occurred to me that I didn't know his name, or his nationality or what sort of companion he would be. But he was taking an even bigger risk because he didn't know for sure that I really knew the way.

In the morning, we met at the agreed point before sunrise and we looked out on the wilderness, pale and shadowy in the first light of dawn and stretching as far as the eye could see into the distant Judean hills. We set off down the goat tracks which began the descent from the Mount of Olives to the wilderness. It was difficult to converse as we walked single file along the narrow tracks, and it was good not to break the silence as the sun rose and the hills began to glow and life was restored. A Bedouin emerged from a tent, a shepherd boy called the sheep, a camel coughed, otherwise all was still. I imagined Jesus on his long walks, single file and silent, absorbing the signs of life into the contemplative silence the Western world has lost. Eventually, we rested in the shade of some rocks, drank from our water bottles and spoke for the first time.

His name was Gunther and he was a German. At home, he worked for a mountain rescue organisation. He flew to remote places where climbers were lost or planes had crashed. He acted as the pilot's pathfinder, and he provided emergency first aid when he had tracked the victims. This was good news. He would be a useful fellow to have around if anything went wrong.

"There is one thing you should know," he said. "I am fasting. This is the eleventh day I take no food. Only water." I was astonished and anxious for fear that he should collapse in such a wildly remote place, leaving me alone. "If I faint," he said "give me one of these pills," and he showed me a little packet in his money belt. This made me realise the folly of the man in Jesus' parable who went down from Jerusalem to Jericho alone. Suddenly it was clear that the desert should only be approached in groups or caravans and the humour in Jesus' story (lost on Western minds) was obvious – as if any man would approach the desert alone! How those first hearers would have laughed at such a folly. Now I was caught up in something similar and was on the wrong end of the joke. But why was he fasting, and in the eleventh day?

"I have come to Israel," he said, "to mark the 40th anniversary of VE Day. It is also the day the Belsen Concentration Camp was discovered. I have come to make a personal act of reparation for all that my nation inflicted on the Jews and for all that the Jews have inflicted on the Palestinians ever since." I was awed by the desert silence and my strange companion, and we sat without words, absorbing the Biblical scale of the Judean Wilderness spread before us.

When we continued, we passed disused army trenches and hideouts, without comment. They could have been bases from the British mandate, though they looked old enough to be from Turkish times. On the other hand, our track was mainly along the old Roman road so they could have gone back to New Testament times. Those barren hills had been the scene of conflict for all recorded time. Abraham had come up from Ur of the Chaldees, Moses had sent Joshua's army from Moab, Saul and David had vanquished the Philistines and fought each other, all on those hills. Now we could see Bedouin encampments, goats responding to a boy's melodious call and there was peace in the hills, at last. Under the next outcrop of rocks, we rested again and Gunther continued his story.

"I would not do my military conscription," he said. I refused to bear arms, so I had to do two years community work. I became a hospital porter and learnt emergency health care. Then I went to a Benedictine monastery as a gardener, and there I learnt to keep silence and to fast." I asked why he had refused military training. "It is more blessed to heal than to kill," he said, and we fell to silence. Once again I was in awe of the person and the place and silence seemed the only fit response. We continued, absorbing the peace of the hills that had for centuries, known no peace. The path rounded a rock and suddenly the scene changed. Barbed wire and bulldozers confronted us. A city of concrete, topped by machine guns, was forcing its way into the hillside. It was one of the new Israeli Settlements which claimed the Palestinian land for its new masters. Blocks of multi-storey flats were being built, cranes and helmeted men were at work and armed guards patrolled the wire fences.

We sat down, as much from shock as anything else, and I took out my camera. A man with a gun came over, prodded Gunther with the butt of his gun and said "Move on." I put the camera away quickly, and we moved on. We walked on in single file and sombre silence. Those Settlements were illegal in International law and they were in breach of countless U.N. resolutions. When would the international community enforce the law and protect the Palestinians? And if they didn't, how much longer would it be before Palestinian patience gave way to the violence of despair?

After a while my companion, quoting Jesus' parable, said "we have fallen among thieves," and I, remembering the story said "and we are passing by, on the other side." "I know, said the German. "Zat is vy I fast."

Saturday-Sunday,
11-12th May 1985

Young and Daring

The most surprising things happen in Jerusalem and one of the bigger surprises was a breakfast time meeting at St. Georges, the Cathedral hostel, with a young man called Robert Block. The story that unfolded was all but incredible. He had just arrived after *running* all the way from Canterbury! Could such a thing be possible? Yes, he had been sent on his way by the Archbishop whose greeting he had carried to the Pope. He had run across the snow-covered Alps, he had sailed from Bari to Greece and then he had run from Alexandria to Cairo and through Egypt to Jerusalem, where he had been welcomed at the gates by the Dean who had carried the Archbishop's greeting to the Patriach. He had run 1,960 miles in 60 days, averaging a marathon and a half a day, for all of eight weeks. It was part of the International Youth Year for which his effort had raised £2,000 from sponsorship. It should be worth at least ten times that figure. It was amazing he was alive to tell the tale. In fact he didn't even look exhausted and we took a walk up to the Pope's Garden on the Mount of Olives. While we admired the view of Jerusalem he explained that he was from Southampton, that he had a place at theological College starting in the Autumn, that running the 2000 miles had been no problem. "It was the practical things that wore us down," and he told of buying supplies every day, cooking every night, changing currency at every border, changing the wheel (of the support vehicle) after every puncture. All these things were pouring forth when another youth came up the goat track, climbed over the wall and joined us. He was 18 years old, from Belfast, and was waiting to start at Durham University, having earned 'A' levels in German, Physics, Maths and Economics. He had spent his 'gap' year hitch-hiking round the world; and he had 48 hours in Jerusalem before joining a kibbutz in Galilee. These two youths, whose total age was 40, had already achieved so much! It was embarrassing even to think what I would have been like at their age. Unfortunately Robert had to return to the hostel for an official Reception but Oram, the Irish boy, was free so he agreed to accompany me on the desert walk to St. George's Monastery in the morning.

Next morning we met at the Arab bus station at 7.00 a.m. though it was an hour before the Jericho bus moved. It didn't matter. There's plenty to watch in the hectic hustle and bustle of an Arab bus station. Oram made the very telling remark that the Palestinians (though an occupied people under Military control) seemed happier than the Israelis (though they controlled the whole place). He likened it to Walsall playing Arsenal. Walsall feel "we've nothing to lose," and make the best of it. Arsenal feel "we've got to win this at all costs." Profound, yet funny. I like that style. The bus station was as busy as ever, endless tooting and hooting with gesticulating and shouting to match. There is such a small space for so many buses, one of which was being driven neatly into place by a boy who looked about 8 years old, who then got out and cleaned the windows. Nothing seems to surprise people here. When we did start there were the usual chickens aboard, a very active cockerel and two tiny kids. They were skipping around cheerfully. Doubtless they would be on plates by supper time.

We got off at Wadi Kelt, half way to Jericho, having passed the

64

new Settlement that had so angered Gunther two days earlier. Oram, who had arrived with the usual pro-Israel view of things (as I had done) nearly jumped off the bus when he saw the Settlement. He stood up and said "How provocative can you get! That is inexcusable!" He was going to read Law at Durham, "International Law," he said, "and I can tell you now, all this is in breach of international law but no one has got the guts to do anything about it."

The walk in the wilderness has to be single file and is necessarily almost silent. It is more or less impossible to carry on conversations over your shoulder when you need your eyes on the narrow track in front. We stopped twice when big rocks offered shade, and we drank water and talked – but only a little. The monastery came into view at about 10.30 and a breathtaking sight it was, clinging to the rock face, like an eagle's nest. We had seen only two youths and a donkey, on the other side of the wadi. We decided to cross the wadi and climb to the monastery and walk to Jericho along the other side. The descent into the wadi and the climb out was spectacular. The sound of water running and birds singing and the sight of rich tropical growth contrasted with the surrounding wilderness. The monastery was open and provided shade and drinking water from the well. We wondered what story lay behind the men in such a place – they all looked so old. Were they poverty stricken peasants or refugees from earlier conflicts? What would bring people to live in such a remote hide-away?

Beyond the monastery, we could see the hermitages in nooks and crannies of the mountain, with ropes and baskets for food and for messages. Did that mean the monastery was still an active place of prayer and devotion? No one spoke enough English to tell us, but an old travel book said *"on the whole this is a place to avoid. In the middle of the day the sun is treacherous, later in the day brigands lie in wait. Safest between dawn and 10.00 a.m."*

Oram and I looked at each other. It was already high noon and he had to get to Galilee that night to start his kibbutz month. The safest thing was to return the way we had come. He would see Jericho another day. Suddenly I felt responsible for him. He was only 18 years old. What would his mother say if brigands came down from the mountains? Everyone would blame me, and they would be right.

The sun was too strong, the way ahead uncertain, so we turned back, toward Jerusalem, uphill all the way. We were probably on the ancient pilgrim path, possibly the route Jesus and all the Jews took when they went up to the Festival. At least for us there was a bus at the half-way mark. It was disappointing not to reach Jericho but, with the threat of blazing sun and brigands in waiting, discretion was called for.

On the bus, Oram said it had been a great day, but that he was puzzled by what really went on at the monastery. Is the Greek Orthodox faith life-affirming, he wanted to know, or is it life-negating? The same question puzzled me. Not only about Orthodoxy, but about all religions. Humanists and secularists can be so much more positive than religious people. We have something to learn from them about positive affirmation. We are too often known only for judgemental condemnation.

"By the way," said Oram as we approached Jerusalem, "I would have walked on down to Jericho, if I'd been on my own, but I was thinking about your age."

Saturday, 10th October 1987

A Scholar in the sun

Dirk, the extremely clever lecturer in theology, from Ghent University, had found himself a tutor for his studies at the Hebrew University and so he was in the mood for the promised desert walk to St. George's Monastery, and on to Jericho.

I knew he was a scholar and that he spoke twelve languages but it was not clear how he would shape as a walking companion in the desert. He might be a little pedantic. Academics, like lawyers, often are. My worries were justified. His behaviour did rather annoy me. The bus had dropped us at the entrance to the wadi, half-way to Jericho, and immediately he tried to find every track on a map and, as we were largely on goat tracks, that was a forlorn hope, but took a lot of time, mostly standing still in the sun which was foolish. He also kept talking about food, with which he seemed to have some obsession and which doesn't interest me at all in hot countries, least of all when trekking in the Wilderness. He had a much larger than necessary pack which included a huge camera which he kept focussing – more standing still in the sun. Also in the pack was a black umbrella, telescoped to small size. "What have you got an umbrella for?" I ventured to ask. And, sure enough, the reply was "In case it rains." Very few people can be radical in theology and behaviour, it seems. An umbrella in the desert "in case it rains" must be the ultimate in caution and conservatism.

Eventually he agreed to let me set the pace and follow the trails I had come to know quite well. We reached the monastery after an hour and a half. At the door, a notice told us that men in decent clothes could visit until 1 p.m., so we pulled trousers over our shorts, to avoid offence, and gained admittance. But inside, on the chapel door was another notice :

> "No singing of hymns
>   or prayers in this Church.
> Only the prayers of the Orthodox
>   to be allowed.
> No Confessional conflict in this
>   Holy Place."

Dirk was utterly reduced by this and wouldn't go into the Chapel at all on those terms and treated me to a torrent of criticism of Orthodox theology which he regarded as a complete denial of the Incarnation (because of its refusal to be involved in the world) and a complete denial of our humanity (because of its repressive attitude to women and sexuality). This last was underlined by the fact that the monks would only allow cockerels, not hens, in their yard! What use are they, alone?

It was very sad to think of all those Christians who would plod and trek incredible distances through Jewish and Moslem land, only to reach that remote Christian outpost to be greeted by the clear statement that their prayers were not welcome.

Inevitably, this led Dirk to issue another avalanche of criticism this time against the monastic life in general because of its retreat from the realities of the world, and against the Orthodox in particular because of their flat refusal to make any concessions, compromises or creative contributions to any form of Ecumenism. It made me feel more at peace with our broad Anglican tradition which we often under-value.

It was at this very same place on an earlier visit that the young Irish student, Oram, had asked whether Orthodoxy was life-affirming or life-negating. Dirk was in no doubt how to answer that.

He was in a bit of a huff when we left the monastery to begin the long trail down to Jericho and soon I was in an even bigger huff. The trail had become an Israeli National Park. Sign posts had appeared. There were painted arrows on the rocks; red for one grade of walk, white for another. The sense of venturing in The Wilderness of Our Lord had vanished and the Israeli presence was more evident than ever, right to the door of the monastery in the desert.

The sun shone strongly and it was necessary to cover the head and drink water frequently, but it was not the destroying heat in which the very air seems to burn. Dirk said that wind is called (in the Hebrew) "ruarch", which was the original O.T. name for the Spirit of God; a consuming fire. A destroyer. There followed a good deal more theology about the ruarch and Dirk asserted that modern Dutch Calvinism had abandoned its hell-fire view of such a punitive and destructive deity. He also said that the Arabs had a name for that wind which, being interpreted, meant "50 days" because it blows for roughly 50 days a year. We agreed the Hebrew was a good deal more descriptive.

This land of contrasts had two more contrasts in store for us as we approached Jericho in the early afternoon.

The first came as we approached Herod's Jericho (New Testament Jericho to us) with its famous archaeological site laid out before us. There, living in the ruins of Herod's Great Palace, were today's refugees. It was just possible to see where Herod had his inner and outer court, where he kept his harem and where his tropical gardens and swimming pool would have been. It was now occupied by goats, geese, chicken and countless children from homes of rag and sack awnings. Many Palestinian refugees had made their way across the river into the land of Jordan, but those who remained were trapped. Jordan had closed the door to a further influx, and Israel refused them the 'Right of return', in spite of dozens of UN resolutions requiring it. So here they remained. It was quite eerie to see today's refugees in the very heart of Herod's palace. Did the inhabitants have the slightest idea of the significance of the place?

The second contrast concerned our welcome in Jericho. When we completed the long trail, the first habitation was a tumbledown hut, which doubled as a shop of sorts. It was difficult to see what trade the owner could expect there. The old fellow got quite excited and sent his boy to bring two chairs which were put in the little spot of shade. "You Ingleesh?" he said. I answered that we were (even though Dirk wasn't) and "Welcome, welcome" followed, with many handshakes. Then the boy was sent to fetch an enormous fan which was battery driven and directed straight at us – a very good idea. "Ingleesh very nice," he said. Then we were offered whatever we wanted from his store. I had an ice cream and Dirk had a bunch of bananas (much better choice). He seemed to want us to have them as his hospitality but we insisted on paying, though in my case it was only 30 agrot (10p) and in Dirk's case 1 shekel (40p). At this point Dirk's Arabic came in useful and we gathered the story of his days in Jerusalem during the British Mandate; of his flight from Lydda in '48 when the State of Israel was formed; his refusal to cross the Jordan and leave his homeland; and his life as a refugee in his little hut, ever since. He showed no sign of bitterness, which confirmed my earlier conclusion that the traditional Arab is content if he can rest under his own fig tree, taking his own time, leaving fame and fortune to others. We thanked him thoroughly and, with many more handshakes, wished him and the boy well.

The contrast came within 200 yards of the Palestinian and his hut. He had showed us a short cut through the stony wadi – and there we were at the big restaurant on the main road – which serves the Israeli soldiers from the nearby military base. We had half an hour to wait for a bus and so we went to the restaurant, ordered a fruit juice and sat down. "What do you eat?" said the barman. "Just drink," we said. "No drink unless food," he said. This annoyed me and so I went out and sat down on the patio by the main road. He followed. "No eat, no sit down," he said. I was trapped and furious. I couldn't possibly stand in the sun for half an hour after 4 hours walking but I didn't want to eat at his place or pay his inflated prices. In the end, Dirk ordered a kebab and fruit juice for himself, and a bottle of water for me. He paid 15 shekels, more than £5. At least it earned us a seat.

We should have gone back to the hut and to the old Palestinian with his fan, where we could sit in the shade, chat, and feel welcome, whether we paid or not. It was only two hundred yards but a whole culture away.

THE MONASTERY OF MAR SABA

Saturday, 21st May 1986

Lost in the Wilderness

Somewhere in the Judean Wilderness is the ancient monastery known as Mar Saba. Very few people seem to know much about it, or even how to get there. It certainly isn't on the Pilgrimage route, in fact the tour guides have been no help at all. They've never set eyes on it. "You go to Bethlehem and ask there. It's down some track toward the Dead Sea" was all the help they offered. At Bethlehem, shop-keepers just shrugged their shoulders but one said "Bad men down there. You no go." Another, very sensibly, suggested a taxi driver would help. Yes, he knew the way and he would even draw a map for me but no, he would not go. The road was too bad for his taxi. He suggested we rent a car and that is how Joan and I came to be bumping through the Judean Wilderness beyond Bethlehem in a very small Renault, looking for a track to Mar Saba. It was not signposted, but had three boulders on top of each other, the taxi man had said. We went past the end of the bus route and before long we realised we were hopelessly lost.

The tarmac road had ended. A stony track lay ahead. The car would never negotiate that; no wonder the taxi man had refused to go. We pulled into the side and looked around. Wilderness. We would have to turn back. There was a single dwelling, in the rocky landscape. It looked a bit broken down, tin roof and mud walls. We could ask them the way – they would be sure to know. We wandered over, but stood hesitantly in the doorway, map in hand. The door opened. A woman, hugely fat, stood there. "Welcome," she said, with a big smile. "Drink tea?" We went in to their two roomed home. She put the kettle on a gas ring, and we heard their story.

They were Christians of the Greek Orthodox Church, and they earned their living carving olive wood crib scenes to sell in Bethlehem. They had once owned an olive grove but it had been bulldozed to make way for one of the new Israeli settlements, so they had lost their home of several generations, without compensation. "This happens. Every day it happens." Her husband had carried away as much of the wood as he could, and it was stacked at the side of the house. He continued his craft, in their 'spare' room and at the moment he was in Bethlehem making a delivery. They had once had a car, a television and a fridge. Five sons had worked in the business. Now they had only the furniture he had made and the children were dispersed – to California, Jordan and Leningrad. We told her we were also Christians – Anglicans. She had never heard of Anglicans. We tried to explain 'Archbishop of Canterbury' but she did not know there was an Archbishop of Canterbury. So we just settled for 'Christians'. After tea, when we were leaving, full of gratitude, her husband returned, riding a donkey. This meant more tea and listening to the story a second time and admiring his workshop in the 'spare' room. We said our farewells with warm handshakes and big kisses (men only) and left, a little shocked by what we had seen, and a little hurt that they had never heard of Anglicans.

We still didn't know the way to Mar Saba, so we turned back and at each corner we saw Israeli soldiers, clothed in military might, protecting the new settlers who were wary and anxious and carrying guns to their fortified homes. We recalled our new friends' parting words. "They can take my home. They can not take my faith, and they can not take my love of my land. So I can be happy. They can not." It was Arsenal and Walsall, all over again.

We had wanted to learn something about Desert monasticism and the ancient faith of the fathers. We hadn't even found the monastery. But we had learned a lot about the trials and tribulations of the modern faith in Occupied Palestine.

We understood why the Christian population of Bethlehem, once 80%, has fallen to 20%. And how ironic it will be if in the place of Our Lord's birth the Christian presence disappears. But can anyone blame them escaping the humiliation of Occupation? It must take a very special will, and faith, to stay.

Saturday, 6th September 1986

The Monastery of Deir Hajlah

The desert monasteries of the Holy Land are fascinating me, for several reasons. One is that they used to be so powerful, housing thousands of monks, and now they seem so weak with but a remnant surviving. Another reason is that they are so hidden away, their existence scarcely acknowledged by anybody. Some people say they survive because they are useful to the Israeli occupying military. From their mountain viewpoints they see who is going where. That is hard to believe. Israeli military lookouts, with sophisticated radar systems, sit on all the high points throughout old Palestine. They don't need a few old monks to do their surveillance. Others say the monasteries, which are all Greek Orthodox, are allowed to continue as long as the Greeks, who own massive sections of Jerusalem, continue to do favourable land deals with the Israeli Occupiers. The Orthodox Church, unlike the Catholics and the Anglicans, has never encouraged Palestinian leadership. Their allegiance is to Athens, not to Palestine. Others say the monasteries continue in name only and that they are actually little prisons to which erring monks are sent as a penance. The uncertainty adds to the mystery, and the interest.

One of these hidden monasteries is right on the edge of the Jordan river. It's called *Deir Hajlah* and it marks the traditional place of Jesus' baptism. These days it is open to pilgrims only one day a year, immediately following the Orthodox Christmas, to celebrate the Baptism. It was time to go looking. And as it's supposed to be on the way to Mar Saba, maybe we could find both, in one day.

The little rented Renault and Rodney, a learned Lutheran from Germany, were duly collected for the search. I had met Rodney, at the Lutheran hostel in the Old City. He had said he was an experienced traveller, that heat never affected him and that he would love to join in a search for the old monasteries, so off we went. Deir Hajlah was not marked on any map, no guide book referred to it and the leaders of tour parties had shrugged their shoulders when asked about it. Only Samir, the Cathedral taxi driver, had been of any help, and he had not been there since the Israeli occupation twenty years earlier. "It is in a military zone," he declared. "Be careful. They shoot first and ask questions later," he warned. However, he could tell us the way. "Leave the road when it turns toward the Dead Sea," he said. "There is a dirt track toward an Army base." So we set off on the long descent into the Jordan Valley, realising that we might not find the place, but intent on enjoying the search.

It was so easy, by car, to deviate from the main road and the first place we sought and found was the supposed burial place of Moses 'Nebe Musa', in the wilderness, overlooking the Dead Sea. For generations, it had been a place of pilgrimage for Moslems and the pilgrim hostelry still surrounded the site, though now falling into ruin. Barefoot, we walked round Moses' tomb, massive in scale and significantly larger even than the Jewish tomb of David in Jerusalem. The puzzle to me was that the Moslems should honour Moses, the man who led the Hebrews to within sight of the Promised Land and who ordered Joshua and his army to take it for the Jews, slaughtering "every man, woman and child, both young and old." That he should be a Jewish hero, I could understand. That he should be a Moslem hero, I could not. Rodney was no help in the matter, though he was a student of the Scriptures. He made me realise the extent to which people are inclined to accept the Old Testament as it stands without question, even when it attributes the most violent acts to God, acts which are more suited to the Devil. It is a mistake to treat the Bible with such holy deference that we fail to see the sort of God it portrays. The invasion of the 'Promised Land' and the slaughter of those who lived there was whole-scale ethnic cleansing. If God is like that, lead me to atheism! People may be like that, and they use God as their justification. They are mistaken and we are equally mistaken, all these years on, if we continue to believe God doled out land as if he was a dealer in Real Estate. It was useful propaganda to cover their foul deeds, no more and no less. This is my reason for coming back to the Holy Land again and again. It never ceases to enlarge my understanding of the Bible. It widens my horizons. It shows why the Old Testament is still centre stage in the modern world's political and economic life. A Third World War is far more likely to spring from the way the Old Testament is interpreted than from the East-West conflict. Biblical and Koranic fundamentalists are as dangerous as each other.

Of all this I became convinced as I padded barefoot round Moses' tomb on the edge of a military reserve in the wilderness. Yet Rodney, a Biblical scholar, continued to say *"It's in the Bible,"* as if it was the mantra that ended all debate.

After these musings in the sun-baked wilderness, we headed further down into the Dead Sea cauldron, leaving the main road and following an unsignposted dirt track. The heat was so great that a procession of camels crossing in front appeared to be rubber legged, the lower parts of their bodies shimmering in the heat haze and not quite joining with the upper parts of their bodies unless, of course, we were beginning to hallucinate. Remembering Samir's warnings, I drove cautiously and, at the first sign of a military base, halted and got out. There were the remains of a barricade, a military flagpole and rostrum, a broken down open-air bar and a sign saying in three languages "Disco Tonight". Anything less likely in that deserted spot, it was difficult to imagine. We drove on, even more slowly, not only because the stones in the path were turning to boulders but also because we imagined ourselves to be under surveillance from some military observation point. The German said that, if a shot was fired, we should stop immediately and get out with our hands up. We hoped it would not be necessary.

The monastery building shimmered out of the haze, white domes and stucco walls and dogs barking. And, all around, the desert wastes. The cleft in which the Jordan river trickled could be seen in the background and the metallic silver of the Dead (salt) Sea glinted to the South. The ground burnt under foot and there was no shade in which to park the car. In the monastery compound, all eyes turned to us. A child who had been playing stopped playing, and a child who had been crying stopped crying. Two Greek women, all in black, who had been hanging washing on a line, stopped. After what seemed a long while, a man who had been building a wall came over and said "Passport". With presence of mind, I had brought mine and produced it from my little day pack but, with absence of mind, the German confused things hopelessly by saying he hadn't brought his and he wasn't British but "Deutsch". Then two or three men gathered and looked at us from all angles. We would burn alive if not allowed to move so, to break the deadlock, I said lightly "Him" – pointing to Rodney – "Heil Hitler". And then, pointing to myself, "Me. Winston Churchill". Then, hopefully, I added "Bang, Bang" and the German got the idea and went down on his knees. With that, everyone laughed and the fat Greek women, all in black, restarted putting the washing out. For some reason the nonsense had worked and we were led through a courtyard of vines toward the Chapel, and the shade.

When we had finished admiring the Church where a hundred candles burnt, adding to the heat, we looked out of the window across the Jordan River toward Mount Nebo, where Joshua had assembled his army for the invasion of Jericho, and then we were shown into the cooler courtyard for coffee. It was surprising to see such an apparently normal life proceeding in that remote desert monastery. There seemed to be enough children for a small school; which was strange for a monastery. But I didn't understand the culture and no one knew enough English to explain anything, though they kept pointing to a calendar with 7th January highlighted. Obviously that was the day they were open and expected visitors. We sat in heavily carved Episcopal-style chairs, much cushioned, and drank the cold water enthusiastically and the hot coffee politely. Also on the table, between the salt and the sugar, was a snake preserved in a jar of fluid and, on the next table, two scorpions and a bigger snake. "We've only got a small snake," I said to Rodney, to break the silence. "Ah! but we've got Saint Thingummy," he said, and pointed to a skull hanging in the doorway. It was all a little bizarre and the black cats added to the sense of the macabre. One cat had caught a bird and was carrying it around in its mouth. The poor creature, eyes wide open, was making neither sound nor struggle and seemed to have surrendered to its sad fate. I was aggrieved on the little creature's behalf, the more so as no one seemed to take the slightest notice. In England, the bird would have been released in no time, but I knew it was not my place to interfere. The cats were probably kept for that purpose. So I drank my coffee, staring scorpions in the eye and listening to the crunching of the little bird's bones.

Rodney hadn't said much and was becoming ponderous. I recognised the classic signs of dehydration. He carried no water, saying he had packed the bottle for the journey back to Germany, which seemed more than a little ridiculous as we were in the desert for a day. He couldn't make up his mind about going to look for the monastery at Mar Saba, as we had planned, so I took matters into my own hands and headed back to Jerusalem. The prospect of having the 6 foot German go funny on me did not appeal. And it was quite likely that, as he was already showing strange symptoms, we would both be up a wadi without any water, within the hour. On the way back he never spoke and, as he stumbled off at the end, it was clear I had done the right thing.

In the evening, we met at his hostel for some fresh fruit and bottled water. He was returning to Hamburg next day and he said he had never felt better. "I've always been good in the heat," he said.

Monday, 8th September 1986

Ein Fashka … Dead Sea

Mar Saba's monastery, fifteen centuries old, was the object of the day's journey. It was hidden in the desert hills, somewhere near the Dead Sea in the Judean Wilderness. Over the years, three efforts to find the place had failed. This time … The rented Renault would make the journey easy and John, the St. George's Cathedral organist, would make it pleasant. That was the plan. Maps were of little help because the whole area was shaded as a 'Military Zone'. We headed first for Ein Fashka where the Seven Springs pour down from the mountains into the Dead Sea.

The sun was merciless but the oasis gave shade and the seven springs cascaded over the rocks, bringing an abundance of fish. They were flowing downstream in such shoals that anyone could have put a bucket in the water and gathered as many as they wanted. But it was interesting to watch because, when they neared the sea, they put on their brakes and turned to swim upstream, against the flow of those coming down. They knew they were swimming for their lives, because the sea was the Dead Sea, where nothing could survive.

It was while I was watching this little drama, with one foot in the sterile waters of the Dead Sea and the other in the living water of the stream, that a stranger came into sight. He was wearing nothing but a G-string, and thick black mud covered his graceful body. Dead Sea mud has special properties which are good for the skin, and a great many people come to be expertly massaged in it. His smile flashed charmingly out of his muddied face. "Watching the fish?" he asked. I explained that they were changing direction to save their lives. At that moment, it was causing a great pile-up. "The fight for survival always causes chaos," he said, "and it's not helped by religions," he added, with strong feeling.

So, with one foot in the Dead Sea and one in a living stream, I was inescapably caught in religious conversation with a nude, clothed only in mud.

He was a dancer from Paris (that didn't surprise me) and he was a Jew (that did). He had founded an Arab-Israeli Theatre of Music and Movement. Arabs and Jews had worked together for several months, breaking down all manner of cultural barriers and producing a show of which they were all proud. Now the whole enterprise had been stopped by Orthodox Jews (horrified by this display of the human body) and by strict Moslems (who saw the show as Western decadence). I listened, but it was getting too hot. "Here," he said, "have some mud; 'nothing quite like it for cooling the blood'!" and he poured it over my head and shoulders. It caked hard, and he continued. "The purpose of religion should be to discover the Spirit that is in every man." That thought was familiar. It was basic to Jesus' outlook. "It's meant to unite, to heal, to liberate." And he massaged more mud into my back. "But the mainstream religions do the opposite; their rules and regulations destroy that Spirit." Jesus' life-and-death struggle with the Jews had been on this very point. "I stand outside most mainstream activities," he said, and he stroked his muddied hair elegantly. "Creeds and doctrines are no help; they only hinder the Spirit within. Religion begins from the heart and bursts out. Not from the head. And it cannot be forced in."

By now, he was standing with both feet in the stream of living water and the fish were dancing round his toes. I was standing in the sterile sea, and the salt and the sun were taking their toll. Then this strange figure went his way upstream searching for the spring, smiling, but saying how sad he was that his reconciling work among Arab and Jew had been stopped by religious people. "They stand," he said "in a Dead Sea."

The Israelis were developing the Ein Fashka Springs as a health spot and in addition to the Dead Sea mud massage specialists, there was pure spring water for all. We bought a couple of bottles and sat in the shade. After a while, it was time to turn our minds and the little Renault toward Mar Saba. "Do you really want to go?" said John. We were both feeling the heat. And it was getting late, too late to risk getting lost in the Wilderness. The Seven Springs and the youth from Paris were enough for one day.

The fascination of the Holy Land is that the things which happen and the people we meet often make a great acted parable. Today was one of those days, even though the mysterious Mar Saba remains hidden, for another day.

Thursday, 11th September 1986

In a time warp

Today was the fifth attempt to reach Mar Saba. Joan and I had got lost in the hills, John and I had become exhausted at Ein Fashka and Rodney the Lutheran had succumbed to heatstroke at the place of Baptism. It was time to hire a car, go alone and go direct. The way was known as far as the monastery of St. Theodosius, beyond Bethlehem, where the bus terminated. The monastery was bolted and barred but a shopkeeper nearby pointed and indicated a right turn soon, which was helpful. The first right turn led to a better road which seemed to be a good sign, but turned out to be a bad sign. A military man appeared from behind a fence and asked where I was going. "Mar Saba," I said. "Are you mad?" he replied. "This is a mine field." I should have known that good roads lead to Israeli army camps, not to Christian monasteries in the Wilderness.

The reputation of the mountain paths around Mar Saba is of "bad men down there". The legends spring from a man called Abou Ghosh who seems to have been the 'Robin Hood' of his day, nearly two hundred years ago. He became a local hero and was known for the customary Arabian courtesy he showed all the travellers he robbed, "the mildest man who ever cut a throat." The bodies were pushed into the ravine and the profits fed a thriving mountain community around the monastery. It was a relief when, from a high and dusty ridge, the twin towers of the monastery came into view, with the Kidron Valley below and the glint of the Dead Sea beyond.

Inside, a monk brought coffee and Turkish Delight and showed me the extraordinary buildings which hung like tentacles over the Kidron Valley. Fifteen hundred years earlier, the monks had lived in the valley caves, coming together only on Sundays for the Eucharist and to collect bread for the following week. Mar Saba was the only desert monastery claiming unbroken Christian worship from its foundation. In the succeeding centuries, the monastery had grown and become a fortress to protect the endless trail of political refugees and defeated military men fleeing from the latest invader, as well as a centre of timeless Christian stability. In fact, it was so timeless that all the clocks seemed to be wrong. Hours wrong. "Yes," explained the monk. "We live in Byzantine time here." They were not only eight hours awry, which meant that they worshipped all night and slept all day, but they were also eleven days out and it was still August in their calendar. There had been no concession of any sort to progress, so there was no electricity, no telephone, and no transport. And any woman who came into sight was put into one of the towers.

As they were still in August they were observing the Feast of the Beheading of John the Baptist, which meant it was 'open house', guests were welcome. I could stay for supper and talking would be permitted during the meal in the place of the customary readings. In the refectory, there were seven monks and two novices, with the Abbot presiding. One monk looked a hundred years old and horribly run down; the others were vigorous, though the long beards made estimates of age or character difficult. Thick walls darkened and cooled the refectory. Salad, tomatoes, olives, raisins and big beans were on the tables, in wooden bowls. Fruit and Turkish delight followed, and coffee because it was a Festival. When the meal ended, the cutlery was not washed, but wiped in paper and returned to a shelf under the table. I did the same. The plates were not washed, but cleaned with bread which was then consumed. I did the same. Obviously there was a great shortage of that most basic and valuable creature, water, which we Westerners take for granted so thoughtlessly.

After the meal, the monks went off to siesta and the English speaking Chrysostom gave me the keys to St. Saba's cave and other hermit chapels in the gorge, so that I could see the ancient ikons and mosaics. In fact, the weight of the huge keys made the walk to the caves too much of an effort, such was the crippling power of the midday sun and the two hours passed in the shade of a fig tree. Besides, who would want to see ancient stones when across the valley there were goats grazing, sheep straying, donkeys without burdens, badger-like creatures scurrying to and fro, and birds of prey swooping? Lizards shot out from the rocks and stared in the sun as if blinded, before they disappeared as quickly as they had arrived. No doubt scorpions and snakes were not far away. There is more life in the desert than people suppose. I did look in one cave, abandoned by the Desert Fathers 14 centuries earlier. The ikons seemed to be in excellent repair and all was in order for the revival that the monks evidently expected. But it was the shade of the fig tree, that drew me.

In mid afternoon (which was late evening to them) it was time for Vespers. It was a High Feast and so all the candles in the many corona were flickering in the darkness, and the light fell occasionally on the face and robes of St. Saba miraculously preserved, they said, 14 hundred years after his death. One by one the monks filed past and kissed his glass coffin, while incense wafted into the domes and cupolas, crossing the shafts of sunlight and giving the whole place the hazy quality of dreamland.

In the darkness, the rhythmic tones and monotonous repetition were soporific and the whole setting was so unlike anything earthly that it was difficult to know which moments were dreaming and which were waking. This is the special gift which Orthodoxy offers the Church. Its worship takes us to the Gate of Heaven. It lifts us to the transcendent. If only it could recognise that other Churches have other gifts to offer, and that being earthy is also true to the faith of Jesus.

Greater Silence followed Vespers and Chrysostom guided me to a monastic cell overlooking the steep drop into the Kidron Valley where Jerusalem's untreated sewage was flushing down toward the Dead Sea. Clearly I was expected to stay the night. The whole place had a spooky atmosphere, the ghosts of times past seemed close. Who knew the horrific stories these dark walls could tell? They had been there when Mohammed was born. They had seen the Byzantines, the Crusaders, the Turks; they had seen the fall of the Romans, the Ottomans, the eras of the British and the Jordanians and now they were surrounded by Israeli minefields. Dusk was gathering and the idea of driving alone in those mountains, midst minefields and Bedouin tribesmen, had lost its appeal. I stayed.

My cell had an oil lamp, a bucket of water, a stone jug, a chair, a scrubbed table, a chunk of bread and a jug of wine. I settled to write and reflect, looking out through barred window on the Judean Wilderness by moonlight. The rocky valley was forbidding, and lonesome. I hoped my little light would survive the night.

Night at Mar Saba

In the cell,
>*Stone floor*
>*Barred window*
>*Rush bed*
>*Scrubbed table*
>*Upright chair*
>*Oil lamp.*

>>*Hunk of Bread,*
>>*Jug of Wine*
>>>*awaiting me.*

Through the Window,
>*Deep valley*
>*Rugged rocks*
>*Mountain tracks*
>*Empty caves*
>*Night sky*
>*Cold moon.*

>>*Hunk of Bread,*
>>*Jug of Wine*
>>>*tempting me.*

In the night,
>*Shadows shifting*
>*Mountains moving*
>*Lamp fading*
>*Spine chilling*
>*Heart stopping*
>*Devil dancing,*

>>*Hunk of Bread,*
>>*Jug of Wine*
>>>*finished.*

In the Chapel,
 Ancient worship
 Lighted candles
 Silver ikons
 Holy monks
 Prayer and penance
 Christ's presence,

  Hunk of Bread,
  Jug of Wine
   lifted high.

In the morning,
 Sun rising
 Window open
 Mountains golden
 Strangers welcomed
 Tables laid
 Fast broken.

  Hunk of Bread,
  Jug of Wine
   shared by all.

Chapter Three

Watching the World Go By

WATCHING THE WORLD GO BY

15th May 1985

Jaffa Gate

Watching the world go by is one of Jerusalem's special attractions. So much of the world seems to be going by. Sitting and staring is an art we are losing in the rushed ways of the West. Jerusalem invites us to recover the art.

Today I was sitting and staring outside the busy Jaffa Gate where traffic hurtles by at a great rate. Midst the lorries and tourist coaches was an Arab boy, about eight years old, pushing a cart of water melons up the hill to the Jaffa Gate. It astonishes me how young these boys are when they start working. He had a donkey alongside on a rope and the donkey also carried wooden crates of water melons. When the boy eventually got to the top of the hill, two armed Israeli soldiers put the butt of their guns under the wheels, causing a sudden break. Of course the whole lot crashed, the water melons fell all over the place and rolled down the hill he had just come up, the cart pulled the donkey down to its knees and the wooden boxes split. The little boy rushed here and there midst the traffic and saved a few melons but the donkey and cart were blocking the Jaffa Gate and all the taxis were hooting. The donkey could not, or would not, get up until someone loosed the rope, whereupon the whole cart crashed down the hill. The soldiers stood by, laughing. I thought of Gunther, my German companion of yesterday, who would have said "Zat is vy I fast".

16th May 1985

Intimate Club

    I am getting to know my way around the maze of the Old City streets and alleys, and today I came across a place that was new to me. It was called a 'Tabasco' and it had a chalk notice outside, in three languages. The English version said "Intimate Club" and added 'cheep beer'. It was down an unlit alley and I tripped on the way in because there wasn't much light inside or out. The 'intimate club' was downstairs, in a sort of cavern. Music blared, very loudly, though it was so dark I couldn't see the speakers. It really wasn't my scene, but I sat at a table, ordered a beer and it really was cheap – less than half the hotel price. But there was no glass, I had to drink straight from the tin, which I do not do well. It makes me feel self-conscious. It was clear this was some sort of a den of iniquity and the burning joss sticks convinced me that drugs were passing round, which wasn't my scene either. It was best to appear nonchalant and remember that Jesus was accused of being a wine bibber and keeping bad company and that he had once told the self-righteous that prostitutes would get to the Kingdom of Heaven before them. Gradually my eyes got accustomed to the lack of light revealing walls covered with international graffiti, among them "Keegan is King". I expected it was from his Liverpool days, but hoped it was from his time with us at Southampton.

    Suddenly, six Israeli soldiers burst in, and questioned everyone except me. The eight Arab customers were made to stand facing the wall, with their arms stretched out. They looked like the back of crucifixions. Their pockets were emptied and the soldiers checked all the documents and used the butts of their guns, and laughed a lot. None of the Arabs spoke. The music continued to blare out. I sat there, drinking my beer in a corner. One soldier dropped some of the papers and an Arab bent to pick them up. The soldier stamped on his hand and two others put their guns in his ribs. Then their shirts were pulled over their heads to make them blindfold. It seemed the lighted cigarettes were going to be pressed into their backs and the New Testament words "Tell us who hit you, who hit you?" came to mind. But they answered never a word and, after a while, the soldiers left, without acknowledging my existence – which I didn't mind in the least. Then all the victims resumed their game of cards and laughed and chatted as if nothing had happened, though one had bleeding knuckles which another covered in an Arab headdress.

So that was why the beer was so cheap in that place! It was like the Jerusalem Jesus had known. It was an occupied city then, and it was his own people who were subject to the sort of humiliation those Palestinians had just suffered. So, before leaving I asked for a graffiti pen. They brought one and crowded round to see what I would write. There was a little space near 'Drink varnish – it gives a lovely finish'. Alongside 'Jesus woz here' I added 'His Spirit is with us'. The one who interpreted English busied himself explaining this to the others and they all shook my hand and said "You good man" and brought me another tin of beer, and I said "You good man too" and everyone laughed and said "Have a nice day" which was difficult as it was almost midnight. But I knew what they meant and it sent me away feeling I had learnt why Jesus went to those places so often, and it wasn't for the beer.

Later I remembered my Saints' supporters car sticker at home. That's a sort of graffiti on wheels. I should have put the slogan on the wall. I'll go back tomorrow. It says "Follow the Saints".

17th May 1985

Decadence and Arrogance

I never feel comfortable at the Wailing Wall/Haram-esh-Sharif and I don't think other people do either. The whole area is just too steeped in the religious and national traditions of opposing parties. Everyone seems to be at their most sensitive, which probably accounts for the massive military presence and the doubled security arrangements.

Until the Six Day War (1967) Jews had been barred from praying at the walls of the Temple, and they had wept for their return. Hence the term "Wailing Wall". After their victory, the Israelis bulldozed all the Palestinian homes in the district and the site was cleared to create the present piazza. A fortress of luxury Jewish apartments had now been built looking directly onto the pride of Islam, the Golden Dome of the Rock and El-Aksa mosques. At this point the two peoples are at their most fervent and the atmosphere is at its most volatile. If any place calls for tact, discretion, peaceful respect (and a quick exit) this is it. So while I watched it was embarrassing to see a group of girls trying to enter the Haram-esh-Sharif above the Wailing (now called Western) Wall. They were wearing shorts and their shoulders were uncovered. The Moslem at the gate offered them blue sheets to drape over themselves to conform with custom. They refused and threw them back, demanding entry as they were. The gate man picked up the sheets and offered them again, but the girls pushed past, giving plenty of lip as they went. All this happened right under the notice which is at all Holy sites, Moslem, Jewish or Christian, laying down rules of respect for each other's traditions. I felt humiliated as well as angry and I went up to the gate man and apologised. (At least they were Australians, not English, I discovered). But, to the Moslem, we are all Christian – and decadent. They don't differentiate between American, Australian or English – all are Christian; any more than we differentiate between Palestinian, Lebanese or Jordanian – all are Moslem. The gateman had been so patient and courteous, the girls so arrogant and rude. What must the devout Moslem think of Christians and the West? No wonder they resist us and our culture.

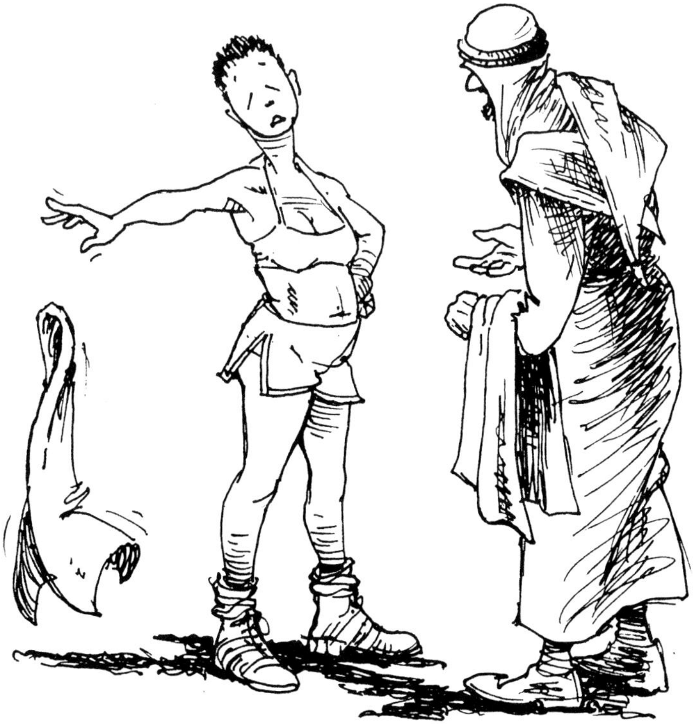

Friday, 24th May 1985

Song and Dance

I have been captivated by the charms of two young travellers. They were sitting at the Damascus Gate, soaking the sun – and watching the world go by. They were young, blond, bronzed and evidently in love.

Usually, I leave couples to themselves. They don't want third parties hanging around. But for some reason I gathered my courage, sat nearby and said "Been here long?" The response was instant. They had been in Jerusalem less than 24 hours but they were shocked and disillusioned. They were hitchhiking round the world, they had been on the move for six months, they had passed through sixteen countries and in all that time they had not seen as much military activity as they had seen in Jerusalem in one day.

"This is what religion does," they said. "It drives people crazy. It creates this madness." At that moment three Israeli soldiers were marching some unfortunate Arab up the steps of the Damascus Gate and into a waiting jeep. Questioning, as they call it, would follow. Another group of soldiers had surrounded three Palestinian boys in the gateway. Papers were being checked. The three youths were pressed against a wall at gunpoint, while they were searched. People were passing by, taking no notice. It was routine.

"We don't need a God," said Soren, with a warm and winning smile. "We just love people," said Bertha, with her blue eyes sparkling happily. "We are atheists," he said. "Yes," added his girlfriend. "Too many wars have been fought and too much blood has been spilt by people defending their God." They were from Sweden and they were staying at a Youth Hostel in the Old City and paying 5 shekels (£1) each. "Why not join us?" they said. "You don't have to be young." The invitation was irresistible, so I followed them through the alleys, marvelling that they had found their way so quickly. I had warned them it was Friday, the most dangerous day of the week in the Old City, but they hadn't understood the significance of that.

The Moslem holy day was ending and hundreds (if not thousands) of Arabs were pouring out of the Golden Dome mosque area, most of them wearing the long white robe which is the garment of prayer. The Jewish Sabbath was about to begin and hundreds (if not thousands) of Jews were making their way toward the Western Wall, most of them wearing black overcoats draped to the ankles, some with black hats trimmed with fur, all struggling upstream against the flow of Arabs coming down-stream. At the very same moment the Christians were making their weekly pilgrim procession along the Via Dolorosa, the leader was bearing a heavy cross, the followers were escorted by brown-robed Franciscans. They were heading for the Church of the Holy Sepulchre. The noise and the jostling of all three groupings rose, minute by minute. On the roof tops, surveying the scene, stood dozens of soldiers; young, tense and looking frightened as they gripped their guns. "What sort of God would want all this fuss?" said Soren sadly. "We don't like Jerusalem," said Bertha. "It speaks of war, not of peace," and her eyes did not sparkle. "The world wants love, not religion," she added.

At the Hostel, I was offered a dormitory place, and as each bed was sheltered by curtains, which gave a little privacy, I gathered my essential goods from the Cathedral hostel and moved in, reducing my costs from £18

to £1 which seemed a good idea, but I hadn't quite bargained for the evening activities.

Alcohol flowed rather too generously, the room was soon filled with a smoke haze (I daren't ask what was being smoked) and the noise grew louder and louder, and a good many arguments were clearly developing. It wasn't the sort of scene to which I am accustomed and the £17 saving suddenly seemed less of a good idea. But one thing impressed me, forcefully. Every time Bertha sang, and Soren danced, the place fell silent. She sang of birth, of death and of love, in English, and the silence was such that it might have been the Elevation of the Host in a Cathedral. And when Soren danced all eyes were focussed, every hand clapped the rhythm. It was as if we were all one.

Later, they sat with me. I tried to tell them, midst all the din, that I liked their song and dance. "Tell me," said Soren, who was all blue eyes, and blond hair, "Your Jesus … did he dance?"

Next Day

Soren and Bertha were moving on to Galilee. They hadn't liked Jerusalem. I offered to show them the Church of the Holy Sepulchre, or the Western Wall, or the Dome of the Rock, but they reminded me they were atheists and said they were not interested in religion. But they did agree to climb the Mount of Olives to see the Holy City, so I led them to the 'Pope's Garden' where we sat on the wall and took in the panoramic view.

"Well," said Soren, "did he dance? This Jesus of yours, did he dance?" That was the question he had posed yesterday, and I had not answered because I had never thought of it before. "You see," Soren continued, "you can not dance and fight," he said. "Did you notice last night how they all stopped their quarrels and their noise, when I danced?" I had noticed. "Dancing is peace," he said.

It was strange to be looking over the Holy City, the home of the three great religions, and listening to two atheists. "We don't believe the Churches, they are for law, not freedom," they said. "We don't believe their morality, it wants people to conform, we want people to be themselves." I wondered whether that was their secret, that they wanted people to be themselves. Was that the special charisma that drew people, including me, as if to a magnet? They wanted people to be themselves. Whatever their secret was, we could do with some of it in the church.

It was evident that drugs had been circulating in the Youth Hostel the previous night, so I asked Soren what he thought about it. "I never touch them," he said. "They mess up lives." I was thankful we shared that view. "Drugs imprison, music liberates," he said, and he went on to explain that when he plays and Bertha sings, it makes their hearts dance. "Your rules and regulations are like shackles," he said. "They don't make my heart dance." I had seen for myself that when he sang they all wanted to sing. He had lifted them through the smoke haze, out of their messed up lives.

At that moment I didn't say much. Listening and looking seemed to be enough. But later I reflected that Jesus had frequented some odd places where he had lifted people out of their messed up lives. He had alienated the religious leaders and lawyers because he didn't like their stuffy ways. He had longed for people to be liberated, not shackled. Maybe Soren was not as far from Jesus as he thought. Maybe he was closer to Jesus than most of us. My regret is that I was so absorbed listening that I didn't tell him so.

We walked down from the Mount of Olives and collected things from the hostel before I saw them off on the Galilee bus. His last words to me were "Yes, he did dance. Your Jesus did dance. It's just that the rest of the world hasn't." And they waved cheerfully.

I made my way back to the Cathedral hostel, only too willing to pay the extra £17 for peace and privacy. And yet I wouldn't have missed the experience for anything. They had made my heart dance, a little. And I would like it to dance a lot more.

October 1987

The Mad Bottle Smasher

It had been a trying time in the Old City. The friends I had come to see were either ill or out of business. I had arrived full of good cheer and was making my way back to the Cathedral hostel rather less cheerfully when there was an unexpected and unwelcome interruption.

Some mad man was in the middle of the street throwing glass bottles, growling like a wild dog, and slobbering like one, too. One bottle smashed in a shop doorway and another on the side of a passing bus. Lots of people were slapping their thighs with laughter, though I failed to see the fun of it and decided to shelter behind a parked car, at which moment a bottle exploded on that very car. About six men approached him but he had a broken bottle in his hand, so they quite quickly unapproached him. Discretion was clearly called for, not valour, and I disappeared down a side street. Later in the afternoon, I chanced across the same fellow again. He was still growling and whining, and about a dozen children were taunting him as they followed at a distance, diving behind cars and heartily enjoying the fun. I guessed this 'bear baiting' was a regular feature, but it confirmed my earlier opinion – even a walk in the street isn't straightforward in this land.

Two days later ...

It's good to sit just inside the Damascus gate and watch the world go by. The café is wonderfully shaded and the oranges which make the fresh juice such a cooling drink are crushed in front of my eyes. The comings and goings are international and unpredictable.

One of the more unpredictable tonight was the growling bear of broken bottle fame who blundered onto the scene. He lurched around, for all the world like Charles Laughton's Hunchback of Notre Dame. When he growled, I feared for his throat. When he spat, I feared for all passers by. Had I been there alone, I would have feared for myself. Tonight he was good humoured between growls and tried to dance for our amusement. Some Arabs from the café opposite led him away.

Three days later ...

There was one thing (above all the others) which had been bothering me so I took steps to sort it out, at least in my mind.

It focussed on the Mad Bottle Smasher. I had seen him almost every day, lurching around the streets with a mob making mocking merriment at a safe distance. One day I caught sight of his face, hugely swollen and blackened as if he had hit himself with one of his bottles, or smashed into some stone pillars. A heavyweight contest would have been stopped before anyone got into that state. What would end this? I began to wonder. Then yesterday, as I returned from the Jericho walk late in the afternoon, I had seen him – flat out on the pavement. Some people had stepped over him, others walked round him, which I did, having a good look at his face as I passed. His tongue was hanging out, his mouth was frothing, blood was in his nose, eyes and cheek and he was both growling and gurgling at the same time. His face was blue black. A man was selling newspapers at a stall not 3 yards to one side, another was selling bread rolls at a mobile stall not 3 yards the other side and another fellow was sitting against the wall offering to clean shoes. No one was taking the slightest notice, and passers-by continued to step over him – most without appearing so much as to look down.

So today, filled with conscience and puzzlement, I decided to wander around the streets he frequented, wondering if he were better - or dead. But the real question raised was – what happened to the sick? So I went along to Nahil at his leather shop; he liked to pass the time of day in conversation and he explained as much as anybody could. As usual, there was not one simple answer but at least three complicated ones, and I hoped I understood them, midst the language complications.

First. Arabs, who became Israelis in 1948 by accepting Israeli citizenship when the State of Israel was formed, received more or less free treatment at Israeli hospitals, if their 'National Health' payments were complete and up to date (which they often weren't).

Second. Those Arabs who fled from the new State of Israel in 1948 and became refugees or displaced people in the Jordan valley received UNWRA cards (United Nations Work and Relief Association) and this assisted them with medical costs. However, 40 years had passed, many had lost their cards and benefits did not apply to their children – only to the original exiles.

And third. The great majority of Palestinian Arabs, who lost their own State of Jordan in the 1967 war and who lived under Israeli rule and occupation, had nothing. They had to pay full costs for all medication, every doctor's visit, every hospital treatment. A doctor's visit was £20 – and one night at a hospital even more, before the treatment began. So medical help for the poor (and in those terms most people were poor) was impossible.

So when the Mad Bottle Smasher had his fit – or whatever it was – and lay down in the street, perhaps to die, there was no point in calling a doctor or an ambulance – as would be taken for granted in England. There would be no one to pay.

So I sat at the Damascus Gate and counted the number of people who, in England, would be in a hospital or a home. In 30 minutes ten blind people passed, some led by the hand, some thumping their way with a stick, most carrying loads of wares they had failed to sell at the Friday market. A dozen people we would call handicapped staggered into and out of the picture and a good few simpletons stood around, spat on the floor, made horrible faces, laughed crazily or whatever. There was one who spent his time perpetually crossing the road at the lights, signalling gratitude to the drivers who stopped, before returning whence he had come – again and again.

Could there be something good in all this apparent poverty and misery? At least all these people were still in the thick of things, among their own people. They were not removed from life and 'Institutionalised' as we do in our kinder and more sensitive society. We don't like to see 'misfits' or such public suffering. We would rather it was shut out of our sight.

Whenever I have a sick hen, I separate it from the others for its own good so that it may have the chance to recover. But it doesn't thank me and never rests till it has got back with the others, even if they peck it to death.

The Mad Bottle Smasher was nowhere to be seen.

5th October 1987

Dining Out

By the evening, the rain had stopped and it was time to go out and have something to eat. I didn't feel hungry but, after so much writing in my room, the exercise would be good. The Old City was dark, and mucky from all the rain and I was the only customer at a rather run-down place with masses of food on display and no one to eat it. I asked for a bowl of soup which was the cheapest thing on the menu (2 shekels – about 60 pence). It was good and I thanked him, whereupon he brought me pitta bread (meat and salad with chips, in a huge open sandwich). I protested because I hadn't ordered it and I didn't need it. "No, No," he said. "You eat. Good for you. My gift. You eat." So I did. It was difficult to imagine such a thing happening on the Israeli side which is more commercially developed. In fact a family at St. George's said they had eaten in West Jerusalem the previous night and it had cost them $20 a head. They wouldn't have been better fed than I was.

On the damp and dark way back, a depressing thing happened. An Army vehicle overtook a Palestinian car and brought it to a standstill. Two soldiers jumped out and pulled the driver from the car. There was a lot of shouting which I didn't understand and the two children in the car began to cry, which I did understand. I stopped and leaned against some rails to see what would happen next. A third soldier jumped out of the Army truck and came up to me. He spoke no English, but signalled me to move on, with the butt of his gun in my ribs. Anyone must have the right to stand still on the pavement and so I stood still, as if I didn't understand. The soldier was only young and perhaps my grey hair overawed him because he gave up and went away. I stood and watched and, after a while, the Army truck drove off and the Arab returned to his car and his children. He gave me a cheery wave and I thought perhaps my silent but stolid presence had helped him.

7th October 1987

I do not get hungry in the evenings. At home it's different, here there are so many thoughts and feelings that eating falls down the scale of things. However, I went into the Old City again tonight. It was mostly shuttered, a few places open, but empty. I went to the usual sad little restaurant and ordered my soup. Immediately a plate of bread and salad came as well. Something similar happened last time. I sent it back as unordered, but again the waiter came. "Please, sir, you have. You eat. It is my pleasure." I didn't look poor or in need. And I make no pretence to be poor or in need. But I keep being given things. I ask no favours, but they come all the time. I had a horrible feeling it was something to do with my age. Whereas in England we might do a little extra for the poor or the young, they seem to despise the poor and leave the young to their own devices but they revere the elderly. That was confirmed when I went to pay. It was embarrassing to pay only 2 shekels (60p) for so much and I would gladly have paid more. He wouldn't hear of it. Instead he shook my hand and said "Thank you, sir. I have respect for you." That was undoubtedly a response to the elderly! Or perhaps it was because, once again, there were no other customers.

During the meal, the lights went out twice – 'power failure' – and gas lamps were lit. On the walk back, which is dark at the best of times, the lights failed completely. It was strangely silent and utterly black in the narrow cobbled alleys of the Suk. Occasionally I passed a pair of soldiers sitting on the street, backs to the wall. They had emergency torches but they looked frightened, in spite of their guns. I walked on but began to feel a bit spooked myself. I came to one impossibly dark passage and wondered whether to go down it or not. The walk back to avoid it was so long that it was easier to go ahead. Straight down the middle, with heavy footsteps and my hand on my wallet. There was no sound except my steps until suddenly there was a great crash right in front of my face and I was surrounded by falling packing cases, boxes and evil smelling garbage. My spine went cold as ice. There was a villainous howling and screeching. I could only think of the Mad Bottle Smasher of a few days ago, who no one would want to meet in a pitch black tunnel. I stood absolutely still and, when I gathered myself together, I realised this was another reason not to like cats.

6th October 1987

Damascus Gate

I do enjoy my seat by the Damascus Gate. It must be one of the most international spots in the whole world. Sometimes I go inside the gate and immediately there is the hurly burly of the market place and a sense of the Orient. Today I was sitting outside the gate and watching the chaos of the traffic and the struggles of the people bringing their goods to market.

It was near the end of the day and people were beginning to pack up their goods. A Bedouin woman was dragging her boxes of unsold fruit across the main street. They were on rollers and she pulled them by rope. The boxes must have been six deep. I could see what was going to happen, before it happened. A car coming round the corner hit a glancing blow and the whole lot went over with the most spectacular crash. They splintered on impact and the fruit spread far and wide. I imagined what would have happened in most countries – the shouting and gesticulating, the cars hooting at the holdup and the police whistling. But here – nothing. The flow of traffic never ceased for a moment, splintered wood or not. No man or boy (and there were dozens around) moved to help or retrieve the fruit. And the woman sat down at the café on the corner and had a cup of tea. Allah wills it. So be it.

105

10th October 1987

Happy Band of Pilgrims

Pilgrims are two a penny in Jerusalem's crowded streets. Often they are in groups of thirty or forty (a coachload) and usually their anxious leader can be seen waving a flag or coloured stick in a rather desperate way. It must be difficult to keep them together midst the jostling crowds and multiple distractions. It's a marvel that more do not get lost or trampled under foot. I just wish they looked happier. After all, these tours are invariably advertised as 'holiday of a lifetime'.

And what do they do? They stand in the sun being lectured, overladen with goods, mouths open, eyes glassy. They stagger up hills and tracks, down cobbled streets. They are whisked away in waiting buses, mouths still open. Torrents of words are poured over them – about Old Testament times, Herodian times, Byzantime times, Crusader times, Ottoman times, The Mandate, The Post War 'Wars', and their mouths sag and their hearts must as well. "Oh happy band of Pilgrims …" they are not!

There must be better ways of preparing Pilgrims and of carrying out Pilgrimages.

Most of the leaders seem enslaved to ritual. They go through prepared forms of prayers and words whether the situation is suited or not. Today I watched one group, some smoking, some chatting, some shopping, one beating a drum, while the leader shouted something about Veronica's cloth – the words lost in the din. These pauses for prayer in the mad bustle of the Via Dolorosa seem the ultimate pious folly. Why not just soak up the atmosphere which speaks louder than any words? Why will leaders not let the Land and the People speak for themselves? The Holy Land proclaims its own message and leaders so easily get in its way.

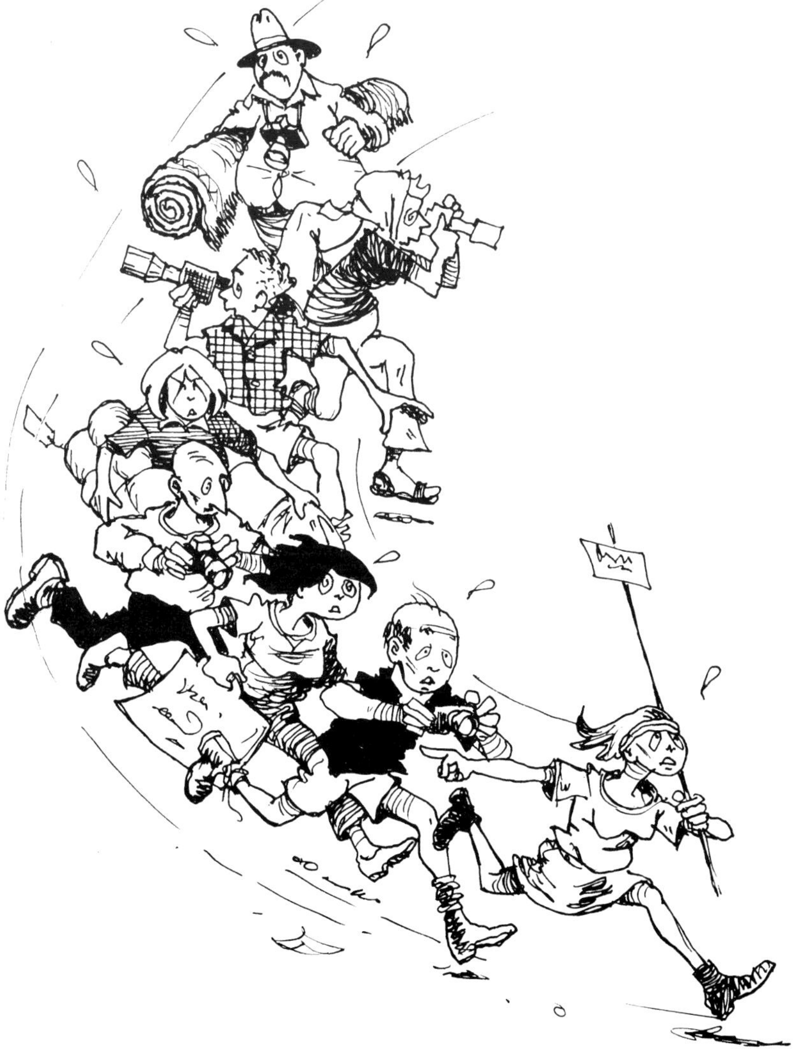

10th September 1997

Land Values

A new face popped up at breakfast today, a young American, full of charm and smiling on the world. It was his first time out of the States. He had just completed a degree in Political Science and he thought it was time he had a look at the world he had been studying. I offered to take him on a tour but he evidently preferred to find out for himself. In the evening I asked him what he thought of the Old City. "Gee," he said, "it's so small," and he went on to speak of his home State of Utah. His father owned a thousand acres which was considered a small holding; most other 'neighbours' owned as much, or more. "Gee," he persisted, "guess the whole of the Old City would fit in our back yard." I knew nothing of Utah or of his back yard but it was true that the ancient walled City was tiny. Viewed from the Mount of Olives, the site where Our Lord was thought to have looked upon the City and wept over it, the whole place looked the size of a pocket handkerchief. It needed no wide-angled lens; the simplest camera could embrace it all. I had often wondered how long it would take to walk around the City walls. It couldn't be tested because of road works and obstructions. Among the obstructions are the burial places of those expecting to be closest to the walls and therefore first in the queue on the Final Day of Judgement, Resurrection or Messianic Arrival, among whom Robert Maxwell was now in pole position. Even so, I had walked half way round the walls, crossed the Kidron Valley and made the long hot climb to the top of the Mount of Olives in little more than half an hour. There was no doubt, the youth from Utah had made a fair comment "It's so small."

I asked him how much his father's land was worth – per acre. He couldn't estimate exactly but he guessed there was so much land around that no one really needed to buy any. "They just come and build a shack and that's how they start, man" was his verdict. I told him the story of Nahil, who had a shop in the 'suk', within the walls by the Damascus Gate. He sold leather goods, olive wood figures and Bedouin necklaces. I had often sat on a stool and listened to his philosophy of life which seemed typical of the Sufi tradition of Islam.

His shop front was no more than six feet wide and the depth of his shop little more than a fitted cupboard, not much more than another six feet. And there he sat, behind his counter, all day, watching the world and its wives pass by, every day. I had never seen him sell anything to anybody and so I had asked him how he made a living. "Living," he had said, "is not making money; it is making friends." And he reckoned that, because of his position in the Suk, near the Damascus Gate, he had friends in every Continent of the world. And as I sat on the little stool, drinking his tea, I could see by the way he was hailed that every Arab passer-by greeted him as a friend, too. He had been sitting there for seventeen years, to my knowledge, and so I asked him when he started there. "As a boy," he said, "my father brought me to sit on that stool, to meet his friends and learn many languages." He estimated it was fifty years. "And now my sons sit on that stool and the shop will be theirs in God's time," he concluded. We continued to talk about life in the Suk until some Israeli soldiers passed by and went up some steps into an arch/bridge above the suk. I asked how the Israelis had managed to purchase a property within the Arab Suk. "Ah!" he said, "a man died without issue and the nearest relative had emigrated to the States. He sold it for the gold." And who had bought it? It belonged to none other than Ariel Sharon. "It was after the massacres at Sabra and Shatila in Lebanon," said Nahil. "Sharon was the minister who organised it. The Israelis held their own enquiry into the murders. Sharon was dismissed and declared 'unfit for government' by the Israelis. But he was not put in prison. No, he came and bought a property in the middle of

Sharon's house in the Arab suk, flies the Israeli flag

the Palestinian Old City." It was the only Israeli property in the Suk. "They would like to buy more," he said, "but no man will sell. Even if they pour gold and more gold until they fill our pockets, we will never sell. My shop is more than gold to me."

The youth from Utah, who reckoned that the whole of the Old City would fit into his back yard, had stopped listening. Well, it had been a long story. A story which introduced thought-forms so new to him that he would not have any experience with which to connect it. As a preacher and a teacher, I knew very well the first necessity of communication – to start where the listeners are. The American was not at the Palestinian's starting point. The values of which Nahil spoke, and by which he lived, and the values the man from Utah knew and by which he lived did not have a meeting point that I could find. And that, enlarged to the international scale, is the problem. Everyone will talk, but who will listen?

Out of courtesy to Nahil, I had not asked him the value of his cupboard shop. Clearly it was beyond cash value to him, but I reckoned that the demand for land was such in and around the Old City that, if Nahil had put a value on his few square yards, it would have been a great deal more than the whole of the American's thousand acres.

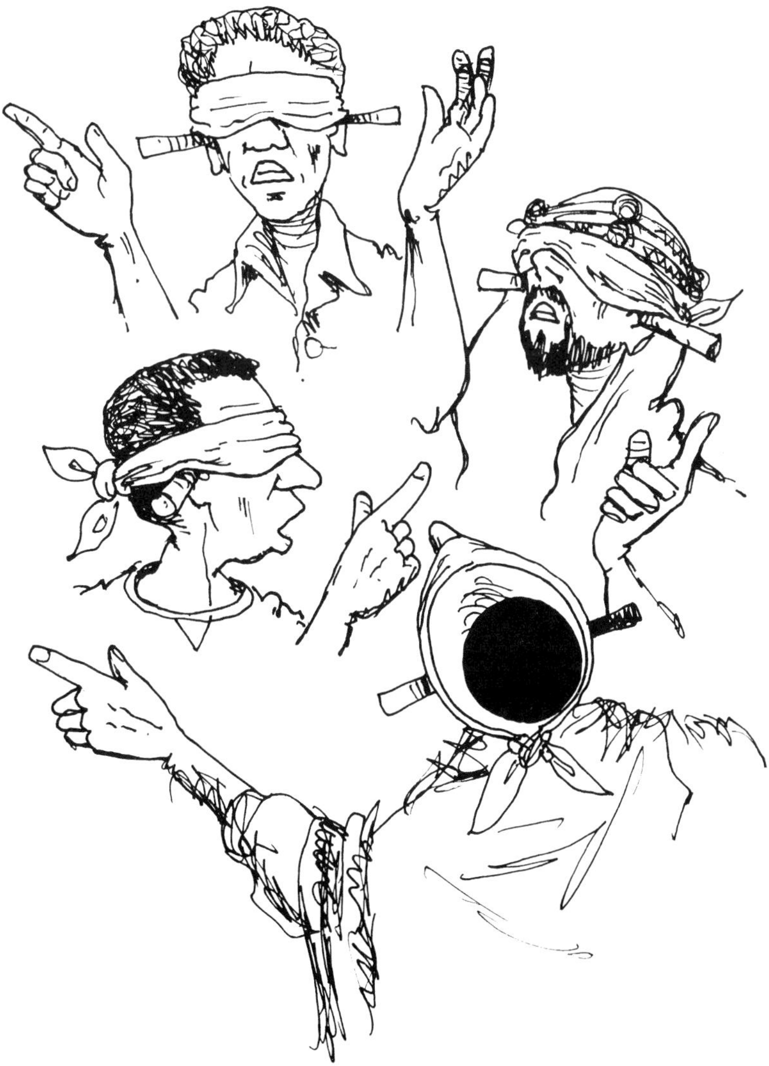

16th September 1997

Palestine Paralysed

For many years I have been in the habit of travelling from the Palestinian bus station each time I go to Bethlehem, or to Jericho. It has been so convenient. It costs about four pence (whereas the taxi would be forty dollars) and the bus station is directly outside the Pilgrim Palace Hotel and not far from the Cathedral hostel. Nothing could be simpler, or cheaper, until today.

This morning I arrived at the bus station early, expecting to visit our old friend, Helen Shehadah, the blind headmistress of the "Al Sharooq" school for the blind in Bethlehem. We have admired her and her amazing work with blind children for fifteen years. But at the bus station, a shock awaited me. It was a bus station without a bus. I asked for the Bethlehem bus. "No buses," I was told. I could see there were no buses there, but logic told me there must be buses somewhere, so I persisted. "Bus to Bethlehem?" I queried more gently, pointing this way and that, which was meant to be a request for guidance which way to go for the bus to Bethlehem. The inevitable crowd gathered, making it impossible to slink away. They all gestured equally strongly, this way and that, and the jabber grew to a crescendo, with several beginning to argue among themselves. Four words in English were emerging all round me. "No bus," which I could see for myself, and "No Bethlehem" which I couldn't believe at all. Eventually a taximan arrived. He, I guessed, would offer me a lift for forty dollars but I would not pay any such figure when I knew very well the bus fare was four pence. I prepared my defiant face and my resistance stance. "Don't you know," he said, in almost perfect English, "Bethlehem is closed. All the West Bank is closed!" I asked what he meant by 'closed', how could a whole town be 'closed'? I had been going to Bethlehem for years and it had never been closed. And then he explained. It was 'collective punishment' by Israeli Government. Ever since a bomb had killed seven people in West Jerusalem, the whole Palestinian area had been sealed off. No one could go into, or out of, Bethlehem, Jericho or any other West Bank village or town. The taximan was depressed. "No business," he said, pointing to his taxi. He was also annoyed because he said it was well known that the bombers who had died in the suicide attack, were from 'outside', not from the Palestinian area at all. "Netanyahu has to show the Israelis that he is doing something, so he does this," said the taximan. "But it achieves nothing," he concluded. So I tramped back to St. George's, saying 'goodbye' to hopes of seeing Helen and 'goodbye' to my desert walk to Jericho. The visit was going to be to Jerusalem, full stop.

What went wrong?

For seventeen years I had been travelling in the Holy Land and, although the politics had often been confused and the conditions difficult, I had never before been barred from entry to a major city. It was evident that far from being better – as had seemed certain on my last visit in 1993 – things had deteriorated to the lowest point in my seventeen years' experience. What had gone wrong?

In 1993 all the signs had been of Hope. New hotels were being built, by Jews and Arabs, a sign of the economic confidence which comes with the promise of peace. A border had been opened and it had been possible to cross from Eilat in Israel to Aqaba in Jordan, a sign of confidence in security. The Palestinians had been allowed to open a Consulate in Jerusalem. It even flew the Palestinian flag. Previously it would have been torn down and burnt. And, in Jericho, the return of Yassir Arafat was welcomed after 25 years in exile. His headquarters were being prepared, the flag flew from his offices and posters of his face, ugly as ever, were in every shop and building and even on the walls of the Israeli Police Headquarters, soon to be dismantled and replaced by the Police of the Palestinian Authority. There were sceptics who doubted, but the overwhelming feeling was one of Hope Now and Peace Around the Corner. That was 1993 and there were more good things to come. The Oslo Peace Accord was signed by Rabin and Arafat, who shared the Nobel Peace Prize to the delight and amazement of Middle East watchers.

So what went wrong? It all turned on two incidents from extremists; one from the Israeli right and the other from the Palestinian left, which together destroyed everything.

The first was the assassination of the Israeli Prime Minister, Yitzak Rabin, who had led his previously fearful people to make peace. The assassin, when arrested, declared that he had done it to honour the Torah, the Jewish Law which said that the land belonged to the Jews as God's gift and any Jew who ceded land to others was a traitor whom the Torah ordered to be killed. The great majority of the Israeli people had been appalled by such language and attitudes and it seemed for a time that the assassination would strengthen the will for peace, though a sinister and significant minority of Religious Orthodox thought otherwise. Rabin's place was taken by Shimon Peres, the leading light in the moves for peace, who had also shared the Nobel Peace Prize. So peace seemed to remain on course, but an Election had to be held.

Then came the second of the two cataclysmic events. In the week of the Election, three Palestinian Suicide Bombers blew up themselves and a number of passengers on a Tel Aviv bus. And the next day, two more did the same in a Jerusalem market place. The new Likud leader, Netanyahu, saw his chance. He declared Peres incapable of guaranteeing Israeli security; he said too many doors had been opened too quickly, and must be shut. Prime Minister Peres and Rabin's widow, Leah, pleaded that extremists who represented a tiny violent minority should not be allowed to put the whole process at risk. But the people voted in a state of shock and, by a majority of ½%, the power passed to Netanyahu. The result shocked even some moderates in his own Party who said that on Peace Issues, they would vote with the Peace Makers – suddenly in Opposition. And so Netanyahu, to secure himself, turned to the extreme wing of the Orthodox Religious, the people responsible for Rabin's murder. It was called an unholy alliance but it kept him in power, effectively ended the Peace Process and has given rise to ever more bombings and killings, the general sense of despair and disillusionment and the closure of Bethlehem, Jericho and all the West Bank.

Oh! what a sad and sorry tale of opportunities lost, of what-might-have-been, of heroic vision halted and dastardly deeds winning the day.

The Church of the Holy Sepulchre

17th May 1984

We were walking the Via Dolorosa, which begins at the place of Our Lord's trial and ends at the place of His crucifixion on Calvary's hill. But it wasn't as simple as that. For one thing, Calvary's hill which was outside the City walls in those days, is now inside today's walls and, to make matters more confusing, it now has the huge Church of the Holy Sepulchre built over it. So instead of climbing a hill outside the walls, we now enter a fortress-like building inside the walls. It's very difficult to get the feel of things.

And if we thought the outside approach was confusing, we ain't seen nothing yet! The inside was one hundred times more so. To begin with, it was very dark. Scarcely any natural light finds its way into the ancient church which seems to be built as a fortress against the latest invader, which is exactly what it has been, many times, in Jerusalem's violent history. And although a million candles were flickering, there was no electric light to guide us. And then there were the crowds jostling and pushing, this way and that. It was like Wembley on Cup Final day! But not so orderly.

There were nuns from Nigeria, black as coal but robed in white and singing choruses with enormous enthusiasm, hands clapping and hips swinging. There was a party of Japanese, jabbering in great excitement and constantly losing their leader who was too short of stature for his flag to be followed. There was a procession of Spaniards, led by a Jesuit priest, candles held high and heading for the Latin (R.C.) chapel; but a Franciscan group, bearing a heavy cross, and following in devotional silence, were heading for the same place from a different direction, and were clearly accelerating to get there first. Meanwhile, the Armenian seminarians, led by their archimandrite, were in procession, singing their evening office with splendid furry voices and a stirring conviction which belied their small numbers, and beleaguered history. Midst all these devotions, processions and the international medley of languages, it was natural to think of the first Pentecost when there were in Jerusalem "devout men, out of every nation under heaven, every man speaking in his own tongue …"

And the number of chapels added to the confusion. I never did count them. There were several chapels upstairs and there were chapels around the walls, for Syrians, for Copts and for Catholics, while the Ethiopians had their chapel, and their homes, on the roof. There were more chapels deep down in the bowels where Constantine's mother found the True Cross, clever soul, and chapels up many stairs, representing the top of Calvary's hill and the site of the crucifixion. But the biggest hubhub surrounded the 'Edicule' where the body of Jesus was laid after anointing. Long queues gathered around, but they weren't queues as English people know them. They were melés, and those with a good shove were making more progress than those without a good shove.

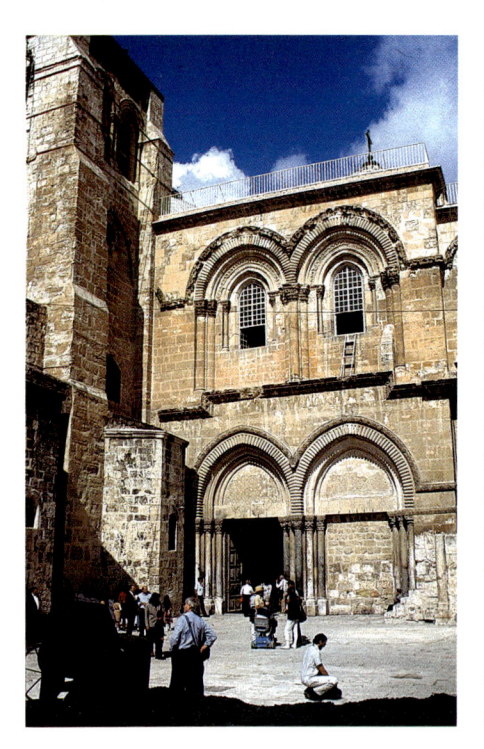

It was easy to imagine the disputes which have raged between the varied denominations of Christendom as each strives to keep his foothold in the central church of the faith. At home it's hard enough for neighbours to share a drive, a fence, or a common boundary. Here the whole building has to be shared, by nations which have often been at war with each other. No wonder the daily locking and unlocking has been done by a Moslem family, neutrals, who have been trusted with the keys for many generations.

It is safe to say that the Church of the Holy Sepulchre is unlike any other in the world.

17th May 1984

The Syrian Chapel

"They could at least have dusted it," said one of our pilgrims. We all nodded in rather stupefied agreement. We were in the Church of the Holy Sepulchre and we had reached the tiny chapel belonging to the Syrians. It was a shocking sight. The ceiling was blackened, presumably by the candle smoke of the ages. Plaster was flaking off the walls, leaving large and crumbling holes. The floor was bare dirt, without the cover of pavers or tiles, just dust. The altar was a rickety table and the glass of its icon was smashed. Was it derelict and abandoned? Was it awaiting restoration? Why should anything, anywhere, have quite such an air of hopelessness? It was particularly astonishing to find such a mess in the Church of the Holy Sepulchre, which pilgrims expected to be the pride of Christendom, and which they had travelled the world to see. It was natural that the Mothers' Union stalwart among us should say "They could at least have dusted it." Didn't she, every week, busy herself in the Lord's house with mop and duster so that all would be clean and in order? It was her way of showing devotion. It was an act of loving service. And there was no sign of it here, where it was most expected.

Cultures were clashing. And we were struck dumb.

Sunday, 21st May 1984

Vive la difference!

My first sight of the Syrian chapel in its state of neglect and disrepair had shocked me and I had never supposed that it was still in use. But when Sunday came and the Syrian Orthodox remnant gathered, it was well filled and the strong male voices sang the whole liturgy without book or musical accompaniment, which was impressive. Some rugs had been unfolded to cover the dirt floor, the altar had been dressed with flowers, rosettes and white clothes and half-a-dozen white robed young servers bore lights but the altar glass was still smashed, the plaster crumbling and the ceiling black. There was no escaping the sense of poverty and despair even though the praises of God were being sung.

Beyond the Syrian chapel, twenty steps away, was the chapel of the Greek Orthodox, whose proud Patriarch alone can claim to be the Bishop *of* Jerusalem. The other Christian churches only have bishops *in* Jerusalem. The Greeks like it to be known that they are the dominant power, the religious rulers of both Holy Sepulchre and ancient city. And to prove it their massive marble-floored chapel is entered through imposing wrought iron gates. A huge crystal chandelier, hanging on chains a mile long, gives brilliant light. The Patriarch, robed in cloth of fine gold and wearing a jewelled crown, is enthroned, attended by a number of priests. The golden censers swing, the smoke rises and surrounds the altar in a haze of mystery and majesty. There is no escaping the sense of

God triumphant and glorious, enthroned in heavenly splendour.

It was puzzling. In a land of contrasts, here was another, at the very heart of Christendom. Syrian priest on his knees in the dust, Greek patriarch placing his golden crown on the altar. Were they worshipping the same God? I have always believed that variety is the spice of life and that in the generous grace of God we can afford to say 'vive la difference' but I had never seen such contrasts in such close proximity. Did they represent the sad story of Christian divisions, were they signs of the hostilities within the faith, for which the Holy Sepulchre is infamous? Or had they a positive message, for those with eyes to see?

On the one hand we recognise the tragedy of Calvary and the Cross, on the other we proclaim the triumph of the Resurrection and the empty tomb. And the sites of both are within this one building. Perhaps it is theologically right that the pain and the glory are here, side by side. We all know that in every human life there are times of misery and despair, 'dark nights of the soul' when all seems grey, grey, tinged with black. And we all know that in those same human lives there are times of joy and celebration when all is sweetness and light and we feel 'on top of the world'. Perhaps it is a superb symbol of these truths that is revealed in the Holy Sepulchre by the Syrians in squalor and the Greeks in glory. They may not know it, but by Divine Accident they are proclaiming a truth together, which neither holds apart. In fact, the follies of human division are turned into divine wisdom in front of our eyes. A death is turned into a resurrection, in the very place where it all happened.

25th May 1986

Liturgical diversions

Sunbeams poured through the Holy Sepulchre cupola, playing like searchlights on the Greek Orthodox worship spotlighting first the censer with thurible, then the priest at the altar, then the Patriaich on his throne, with clouds of incense wafting through the shafts of light and a dozen male voices chanting rhythmically all the while. I decided to suspend my criticisms of Orthodox theology and let the Spirit of worship lead me where it would.

I stood in the midst of five nuns (if not nuns, women in uniformly heavy black). From time to time one went and lit a candle, placing it to burn on a great votive prayer wheel. I was just arranging to offer my candle in thankful remembrance of all the people who have been my strength and stay in life's key moments when another woman arrived at the wheel with a dozen candles and a sheet of paper, with all the names and causes in writing. While she was busy lighting her dozen candles, the paper caught fire and she dropped it on the floor and a man came up and stamped on it and took half the candles off her. The rhythmic singing continued and my mind returned to thanking God for those people who have carried my Cross a little way – my 'Simons'. I was preparing to light my candle, for the second time, when another woman got into difficulty. The 'tray' or 'wheel' was very full and, when she tried to add her candle, she got burnt, dropped the candle and let go a string of expletives and turned to the nuns with a heavy scowl. The rhythmic singing continued but I decided to delay adding the candle for my 'Simons'. After a minute or so, a nun came and pulled a couple of dozen lighted candles out of their holders and threw them in a waste container. The rhythmic singing continued and so did the shafts of sunlight but, if that was all that happened to the candles, I wouldn't bother to light one after all. It was about this time that a server, dressed in scarlet and gold, arrived swinging his thurible and adding to the clouds of smoke. I noticed everyone bow and cross themselves when he censed them. Caught up by all this reverence, I bowed deeply from the hips and was astonished to hear the most unexpected fart. For a moment, I couldn't believe it was me. But it was. I daren't look at the five nuns but stared straight ahead, thankful for the rhythmic singing which continued powerful as ever in spite of this latest diversion.

I'd quite lost the liturgy by now, and my Simons, which was a pity and the fellow in scarlet and gold with the thurible was on his way again. This time I only inclined my head, stiffly. Shafts of light still played mysteriously and I went into a quiet corner of the Holy Sepulchre and made a serious effort to name before God all those people who, over the years, have brought me shafts of light, and led me a little way on, often without knowing it. It is an extraordinary number, and growing. The rhythmic singing continued until it was finally replaced by the thump, thump, thump of the procession out of the Church. The liturgy, diversions and all, was complete but my list was not, and probably never will be.

Outside the Church everyone was immediately soaked in brilliant sun, shocking to the eyes after the interior gloom. It was a signal to stop thinking about all those little lights and rejoice in the fact that together we all reflect the greater light of *'the Father of all light, in whom there is neither shadow nor variableness of turning'*.

Tuesday, 29th September 1987

Life and Death

Inside the Holy Sepulchre, I had hoped for a few moments peace in the cool. What a foolish hope! As I was walking round the 'Edicule' or 'Tomb', near the Latin portion, a woman stumbled and fell, at my feet. She was elderly and had swooned completely away and was utterly unconscious with no colour at all, even in the lips. I quite thought she was dead. A crowd gathered and they all thought she belonged to me, and that I ought to do something. I went and got a Verger who came and looked at her in an utterly useless way. He made a sort of clucking noise, and went away. I then went and fetched the resident photographer, who knows the whole area so well. But he did exactly the same. He went and fetched his father who came in with a big show and a bigger voice, only to do more clucking and head shaking. He went and fetched a man from 'Touristic Police', but by then the woman's Tour Leader (French) had arrived, with a Franciscan, and they carried her into the Latin (Catholic) Chapel. There must be quite a few accidents/illnesses there during a year, but there doesn't seem to be a recognised procedure. A year or so ago an American student told me he had been held up and robbed at gunpoint in the Holy Sepulchre. Prayers and pilgrimage had been going on all around him but nobody had done anything to help him. It was a bit like that today; the poor woman didn't get much help. I asked later if she had died. Nobody seemed to know but somebody said "Wonderful place to go".

Of course it is no good expecting Western norms to apply when we are travelling in another culture. Robert Curzon discovered this when he attended the "Kindling of the Easter Fire" in the Sepulchre a hundred and fifty years ago. In his account he describes the behaviour of the pilgrims as "riotous in the extreme" and that the ecstasy of the faithful thousands, rushing to see the Holy Flame, left 500 dead on the floors of the church. "Many of them quite black with suffocation," he wrote. "Others all bloody and covered with the brains and entrails of those who had been trodden to pieces by the crowd."

It wasn't quite like that today, but it wasn't difficult to imagine.

Tuesday, 3rd June 2003

Guarding the Tomb

The Church of the Holy Sepulchre was empty! Whoever would have dreamt of such a thing? The teeming hordes from every nation under the sun which normally crowd the church and enliven it with hymns and devotions were not there. Not one. It was the clearest sign of the times, and the saddest. The most significant church in Christendom, covering the site of Calvary's crucifixion and the place of the resurrection – empty.

Well, not quite empty. The officials were there, prepared for duty but with no duties to perform. The Moslem 'keeper of the keys' was sitting on his bench just inside the great doors. He was drinking Arabic coffee. A Coptic priest was at his end of the 'Edicule' or Tomb. He was tending candles. A Greek Orthodox priest was sitting on a stool at his end of the Edicule. He looked very bored but his day brightened when he rebuked me for crossing my legs when I sat down. At the entrance to the Latin (Catholic) chapel a brown robed Franciscan was sitting next to a Confession Box. He was obviously waiting for penitents, but there were none.

The silence was eerie because unnatural. My footsteps, though sandalled, echoed. It was even possible to hear pigeons, cooing in the cupola. And sure enough, there they were, dozens of them sitting on ledges high up in the roof. It was the first time I had ever seen or heard them. It was a relief that they broke the silence. It was clear that the priests guarding the shrines were not going to.

The Franciscan looked the most amenable, and he spoke perfect English. At first he though I was a penitent. "No one today, no one yesterday," he said, but he was disappointed again, confession not being my purpose. "It is boring to sit here all day," he said. Not so long ago, they had been hearing confessions at the rate of 20 an hour, which must have meant a bit of a rush for priest and penitent. "If there is a long queue," he said, "I tell them to keep it short." This seemed a strange sort of pastoral care as sins might be many and can be complicated, but it was not for an Anglican to question the ways of Rome, or the customs of the Holy Sepulchre, so we passed to other matters. He was from Ghana where English was the language of education, after which he had been sent to Italy to study theology and philosophy which was examined in Italian. Now in Jerusalem, he had become fluent in Arabic, and literate in Hebrew. He had been resident in the Holy Sepulchre for a year. I had not realised eleven Franciscans lived there, with monastic cells and refectory above the Latin chapel. The Moslem keeper of the keys locked them in each night so that they could do no harm to the property of the other chapels, there being a long and sorry history of theft and even of murder, between the rival groupings. In fact it was the theft of a silver star from the Church of Nativity that was the flashpoint for the Crimea War.

The Latin chapel has a more modern look than the others, which puzzled me because the law of 'Status Quo', which governs that church and all the parties to it, does not allow change. This makes any modernisation impossible, trapping everyone in a time-warp. The 'Status Quo' rules began in the Ottoman period when a Turkish Sultan (evidently a very wise one) did not want to become involved in religious disputes about the building and its use. He persuaded all parties to sign an agreement to change nothing without the consent of all the others. It may have been a shrewd move from his point of view but it has left the church stuck in the year 1757.

Every succeeding government or occupier has seized on the doctrine of 'Status Quo', with relief. It has been re-affirmed by the Council of Berlin (1870) by the British Mandate (1918) by Order in Council (1922) and by United Nations (1948) when Israel was born. No government wants to stir up the international fracas which would follow if one of the nations lost a yard or two of their foothold in the sepulchre. Neither would they want to face the consequences of introducing a new grouping which would want to take a yard or two, or a good deal more. So the Protestant churches, and any others who have appeared in the last thousand years, have no place. This probably explains the "discovery" of the Garden Tomb and its development as an alternative for Protestants. But it did not explain how the Catholics modernised their chapel and introduced an organ. So I put the question to the priest who had no penitents.

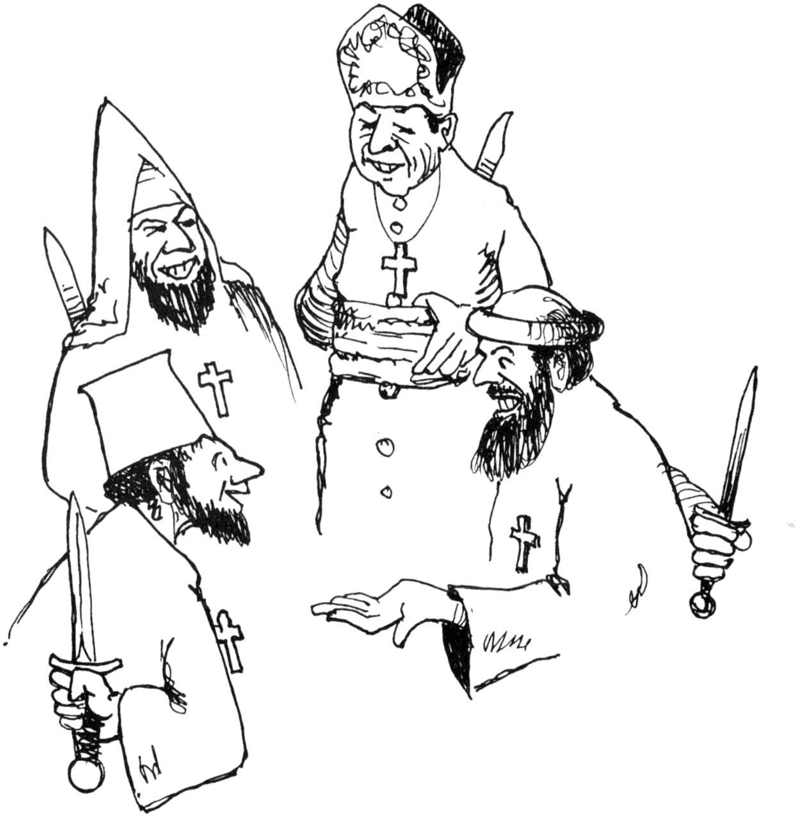

"Ah," said the Franciscan from Ghana, "that was part of the Status Quo." That seemed unlikely and needed to be questioned. "Well," he said, "an arrangement was made that it would only be played twice a week and never when others were worshipping." It would be interesting to know the intrigue by which the Romans pulled that off, and it would be interesting to know what the others think of it now because I have heard the organ trumpeting forth on full volume and, with evident triumphalism, drowning all its rivals – though the Armenian seminarians, in full voice, can make it a close run thing.

But today all was silent. The 'watchdogs' sat, guarding their shrines, each having no trust in his neighbour.

And the Moslem sat, inside the door, holding the keys, presumably the only one they all trusted.

The keeper of the keys

Chapter Four

Viewpoints

THE FIRST INTIFADA

We didn't know it at the time, but we witnessed the beginning of The Intifada. It was not a planned uprising, it was a natural response to an incident we happened to see. This is how we recorded it, at the time.

Wednesday, 28th October 1987

It was the day to meet Brother Cyril, a Roman Catholic monk, who was to show us round Bethlehem University. The University has been established by the R.C. church (here called the 'Latins') as a means of providing Higher education within the occupied West Bank. It is an effort to stem the tide of emigration, the exodus of Palestinians which is denuding the local churches of membership and creating a Palestinian diaspora around the world. There are now more Palestinian Christians living in Sydney than there are in Jerusalem.

There were ten of us in our group. We were shown through the main gates and we were standing around in the compound, waiting for Bro. Cyril and passing the time of day with some students, when there was a shout of excitement and a number of students rushed across the compound. Our hosts gathered us together quickly and we were hurried to a side exit. The students were bolting the doors from the inside and putting up barriers. "Go Quickly," we were told, "there will be trouble," and we were hustled out of the compound and into the street. Meantime, the Israeli army had arrived and soldiers were running in all directions. In no time the University was surrounded. A café owner called us off the street and told us we could have coffee on his roof, which looked into the University compound.

It was only then that we saw the cause of the trouble. Some students had hung the Palestinian flag over the University gates. That is banned by the Israeli occupiers. The flag is seen as a sign of defiance and resistance and as support for the Palestinian Liberation Organisation (PLO) which the occupiers have declared illegal, as a terrorist organisation. So the flag had to come down. From our excellent vantage point we could see the army outside the gates, black masks covered their faces so that they looked like the terrorists. Inside the compound, students hung around. But when tear gas was exploded, they went inside. We stood on the roof for nearly two hours, but little happened. An uneasy quiet seemed to prevail. The flag remained. We went to lunch at nearby Tantur Study Centre.

It was there that we heard the news. Two students had been shot and one was dead. We wished we had not left our vantage point because while we were on the café roof we were probably a restraining influence on the Israeli military. We felt guilty and we wished we had continued our watching brief. It all seemed so tragic. It had only been a flag, but it had cost some young man his life. It seemed so unnecessary, so pointless.

Our programme for the day had to be abandoned so we stayed on at Tantur, the centre for Ecumenical studies and, in the afternoon, we met three lecturers from the University, all Palestinian Christians. They were mourning their student. "He was a good quiet lad. Twenty-two years old. Studying social science. He was doing voluntary social work among West Bank refugees. We have known him many years, all through his school." They feared trouble for weeks to come. "Probably the University will be closed tomorrow, maybe for three weeks. The Army will take over. It is our punishment." They described the raid. "They were Army professionals. They were masked. They were marksmen. They make no mistakes. But they don't care who they get."

A little later the professor who had hurried us out of the compound arrived. He confirmed that the dead boy was Isak Abu Srur, aged 22. "I taught him all through school," said the professor. "He never touched a gun in his life. He wouldn't know how to use it. The gunmen who did this should be brought to trial, but it will be the University which is punished, not the Army. Wait a few days, and you will see," he told us.

We listened to the professor because he was obviously distraught. "Most of our young students go to Paris, Leningrad, California or Amman for University," he said, "and then we never see them again." It was clear that the Bethlehem base was hugely important if there was ever to be an educated Palestinian leadership. "The occupiers do not want us to be educated," the professor continued. "They close the University on any pretext and nearly always at examination time." He was feeling guilty because he had persuaded Isak to stay and not to go abroad. "Oh, if only he had gone to Paris, he would be alive. But I told him to stay. He was the sort we need."

In the evening, all our group and the University staff tried to understand what the Gospel of Jesus has to say in such desperate times. "What does 'love your enemies' mean in such a situation?" I asked. And one replied. "What am I meant to do? When he comes to blow up my home, or to rape my wife, do I say 'That's all right. Carry on. I will forgive you.' Of course not. That is not loving my enemy. That is encouraging him to do more evil things. If I love my enemy, I must correct him when he does wrong. I must tell him. He must know he is doing wrong. The trouble is that it is difficult to say anything to a man with a gun. So resistance is necessary and that brings more violence. Once the spiral starts, who can stop it?"

The Tantur bus brought us back to Jerusalem. We were heavy-hearted. The day's events had shocked us. We had seen and learnt a lot but we were overwhelmed by the apparent injustices and the evident grief of the University staff as well as the students. And all the time there is the terrible feeling that this whole conflict is on a downward spiral and that the worst is yet to come.

Thursday, 29th October 1987

We were warned before we set out for Gaza that there could be trouble.

After witnessing the Army action and the shooting of the previous day, we felt sure we would be able to take anything in our stride. That is what happens to people caught up in all this conflict. It is amazing how quickly the extraordinary is treated as ordinary, the outrageous as commonplace and, in no time at all, the unacceptable becomes acceptable and the wrong becomes the norm.

We were beginning to become blasé about the misery of poverty, the outrages of injustice and even the military execution without trial we had witnessed. So when we were told to expect trouble in Gaza we just said "That's O.K." and got on the coach as if someone had said it might rain.

At the Gaza road block, an hour and a half from Jerusalem, we were stopped and told of troubles ahead. The coach, which had Israeli number plates, would not be safe and could not continue. So we trooped out and hung around in a depressing roadside café until cars with Palestinian number plates arrived from the Middle East Council of Churches, who were our hosts for the day.

Fires were already burning in Gaza. It was a protest against yesterday's shooting, but fuel had been added to the fire. The news circulating was that Bethlehem University was to suffer a severe punishment. It was to be closed for three months, a whole term.

To our group, this punishment seemed near madness. Obviously it would be counter-productive. It would mean all those young students would be even more angry and, devoid of the University work and discipline, would be free to roam the streets and express their fury. Closing the University would invite trouble. It was another example of the way things are distorted and the wrong becomes right. It was the gunman who should have been brought to justice. Instead, the University was to be closed. Injustice on injustice.

The Gaza Strip

At the Middle East Council of Churches base in Gaza, some facts were put before us.

Gaza, a narrow strip of land only 40kms. by 6kms, had become the most densely populated place on earth. 650,000 Palestinian refugees were herded into the world's most crowded camps. Meantime a Settlement was being built to house 2,000 Israelis. They were allowed water for their gardens and for their swimming pools. But the Palestinians were tightly rationed.

The Palestinians were stateless and without Passports. They were not allowed to spend a night out of camp, though 100,000 a day gathered at the road blocks from 4.00 a.m. hoping for a day's labour in Tel Aviv, Jerusalem or elsewhere. If employed, they would provide the cheap labour that was building the new Israeli settlements and businesses.

Military control was absolute. "Here," said the Executive Secretary of Middle East Churches, "we have the policy and the conditions which are a recipe for disaster."

While the sorry story was being put to us by the head of the Middle East Council of Churches, we could see smoke rising from fires in the streets. The phone rang and we were told some of our programme had to be cancelled. The Refugee Camps had been sealed off. There was shooting in the streets. Four of us were permitted to go in a private car to see for ourselves, at close quarters.

The trouble and the anger centred on the fate of a man and his wife with their eight children. They were sitting in the 'midst of their home. But their home was no more. It lay at their feet, a pile of rubble. The Military commander had sent a bulldozer. They had been given one hour to throw their belongings into the street. Then, in front of their eyes, their home had been demolished. That was the policy of community punishment. There had been no arrests, no charges, no trial, no conviction. But a corporate punishment. The hapless family had relatives who had been convicted and imprisoned some weeks earlier. Now the families of the convicted men were being publicly punished. This was the pattern for Palestinian refugees, trapped in the Gaza Strip.

It was an example of a breach of all International Law and convention; of the removal of all human rights and dignity. And we had seen it with our own eyes. How quickly does the outrageous become the norm, the unacceptable become acceptable and the wrong become the right.

Dr. Haider Shafi of the Red Crescent

Back at the M.E. Council of Churches, we listened for an hour to Dr. Haider Shafi, Chairman of "Red Crescent" which sought to relieve some of the medical miseries caused by bad sanitation, inadequate housing, dense over-population, low morale, extreme climate and – worst of all – refusal of the occupying force to allow a hospital to be built or Relief Agencies to enter the area. His was a pitiful and even helpless cry. "We had the land. We had the money. We had the plans, we had the men (to build the hospital). They refused the permission. They put a security closure on the land. Now they have given it to their 2,000 settlers."

Mr. Tawfiq Ghazala, lawyer

By now, we were all concerned about the Law. In England, we are so accustomed to the Rule of Law that we doubtless take it for granted. We are so accustomed to the supremacy of the courts that we can not imagine anything else. Now we were all coming to realise we were in the midst of something we had never known – a society without recourse to the Rule of Law, a society in which the Courts were not supreme. So a student could be shot. A home could be bulldozed. The hospital land could be seized. And no one could do anything about it.

The outrageous could become the norm. The unacceptable, acceptable. We had seen it.

So we were pleased to meet Mr. Tawfiq Ghazala from the Gaza Centre for Rights and Law, and three senior lawyers from his department. They confirmed all the conclusions we were reaching. The 'Military Courts' were a farce. "No courts in any legal sense." The 'evidence' did not even have to be presented openly in court. The 'judge' was not trained in law. The whole proceedings were conducted in Hebrew, though the accused and their lawyer spoke Arabic. The laws on which a person was charged were military laws, published only in Hebrew, and subject to change, according to 'Security' requirements.

Mr. Ghazala's Centre for Rights and Law was powerless, but they collected Case Reports for International journals and provided interpreters in the Courts. It was another sorry story.

As we boarded the buses for the return to Jerusalem, the streets of Gaza were filling with angry youths and plumes of black smoke were rising from the region of the refugee camps. We would begin the journey with Palestinian number plates to avoid the risk of being stoned, then we would change to an Israeli vehicle to avoid security checks from the Army.

Our group was exhausted, and depressed, but we agreed on one thing. When the M.E. Churches Executive had told us that the policy and the conditions were a recipe for disaster, he was absolutely right. Only time will tell what form the disaster will take.

Friday, 30th October 1987

There was a small entry in the Jerusalem Post about the uprising at Bethlehem University, which we had witnessed.

It said that Isak Abu Srur had been buried before dawn in the presence of his parents and a muktar, in an unmarked grave. This was done on military orders.

No doubt it was 'before dawn' to prevent demonstrations and the 'unmarked grave' was to prevent Isak becoming a popular focus of heroism or martyrdom. To my mind, it reveals a State which is paranoid, and riddled with guilt.

Note: That day the fires in Gaza spread and more homes were bulldozed. The Uprising (Intifada) which had begun with a Palestinian flag in Bethlehem, was taking hold all over the Occupied West Bank.

INTERVIEWS

Monday, 26th October 1987

The next ten days promise many things, not least a series of meetings and discussions with people who have been at the sharp end of the Israel/Palestine conflict. There are ten of us in the group, led by "Living Stones," an Ecumenical Trust with Roman Catholic leadership. Their method is not so much to visit the famous sites and see the ancient stones but more to hear from the people, the 'Living Stones', caught up in all the confusions. The first of the meetings, tonight, was with an Israeli war hero....

GIDEON SPIRO, ISRAELI COMMANDO

Gideon Spiro looked as if he had stepped straight from the Army's elite Commando Corps that very day. In fact it was 20 years since he had been decorated for heroism for his part in the 'Six Day War' which had put Jerusalem in Israeli hands. But he had retained the rugged look, strong and muscular in a vigorous athletic way. It was hard to believe he was older than I am. He had not a grey hair; not an ounce of fat on his lean body. He was casually dressed in jeans and a denim jacket which didn't quite conceal his bullet-proof vest.

He spoke to us of the 19 years (1948-1967) in which the State of Israel, newly formed by United Nations decree, struggled to come into existence. He spoke of his unwavering support for that State, for a homeland for the Jewish people, and of the triumphant entry to Jerusalem in 1967 and the glorious victory of the Six Day War which had convinced the nation of its Divine destiny as God's Chosen People to possess and rule the land.

"But," he declared passionately, "that was our undoing. That was the bad seed that would bear an evil fruit. That was the cancer in our midst. What should have been our Triumph became our Tragedy."

He described an experience from the first days of the Occupation. His battalion had taken over an hotel. The Arab staff had fled. He needed to know how a piece of essential apparatus worked, so he went to find the ex-manager. When he found him, the man was terrified, convinced he had come to rape his wife, or murder him. "Do what you like to me," the man had pleaded, "but let my wife and children be." At that moment, he had realised that an Occupying Army had Absolute Power and could do anything without let or hindrance. Military Law applied. He was that Military, and could make that Law. His sad conclusion was that from that day the Occupiers had taken advantage of that unchecked power. He had not raped the wife, but his people had raped the land they had won that day.

He then traced the sorry tale of the 20 year Occupation (1967-87), of the increasingly Draconian measures necessary to control a whole people, of the increasingly heavy taxation falling on those people to pay for their own subjugation, of the complete removal of all civil and human rights, contrary to International Law, and of the steady slide toward a dictatorship as political criticism was suppressed in the name of security. This had led to his own arrest, dismissal from his employment, loss of pension, imprisonment and he was now marked as a traitor and wore his bullet-proof vest because "there are many of my Israeli brothers who thought prison too light a sentence."

His own conflicts with his government had come to the open over the Lebanon War of '82 in which he was one of the officers who had refused to serve. Instead, he had formed a new pressure group called "There is a Limit". In 1982 there had been, he said, a mad wave of nationalism. "A war always diverts attention from domestic failure," he said. "This war was worked up by Begin and Sharon who promised in the Lebanon another "Victory in Six Days", a victory that would "Give The Holy Land to the Holy People for a Thousand Years". He described it as "blatant racism, an orgy of nationalism, a blood letting of hatred against Arabs and, in addition to all that, a political folly which was doomed to failure." Two years later, as the War faltered on and the death toll grew, Begin resigned, Sharon was disgraced, knowledge of massacres brought shame, the Syrians had entered Beirut and the policy was exposed, the cancer was seen. The bad seed was bearing the bad fruit he had forecast. "I knew I had been vindicated. I was released from prison. But I now have to wear a bullet-proof vest for ever."

Worse was to follow! We then heard what we all suspected. That the whole unjust and immoral situation was viable because of American military and financial support on the massive scale, and British complicity. "Without that support," he asserted, "Israel would not last one week." He reckoned the American aid paid for the Occupation and the Lebanon fiasco "so that the Israeli people could carry on with their high standard of living, as if nothing was happening." It seemed certain the support would continue because Israel had become the Western foothold in the Middle East, to be maintained at all costs, even the cost of violating International Law, Human rights and common sense. "Political expedience is the name of the game," but he added, with some foreboding, "There will be a day of reckoning."

It had been a gruelling evening. It had been a painful experience. It was as if we had been listening to a present day Jeremiah. And the situation seemed as hopeless. "Oh! how I would love to live in New Zealand, but my duty is here," he concluded.

Tuesday, 27th October

THE GRAND MUFTI OF JERUSALEM

It was 1,300 years ago that the triumphant first followers of Mohammed the Prophet built Jerusalem's greatest glory – the Dome of the Rock.

"Perfection is more than the mind can take. It turns the heart," said one of our party. "This puts St. Paul's, Westminster Abbey and all those in perspective. They're plain boring compared with this," said another. "The Taj Mahal is totally satisfying to the eye outside but this is totally satisfying inside as well," was the view of the art historian in our group. "This is the centre of the religious world, and it's all glory," said the BBC reporter, into her microphone.

It was in the shadow of Islam's greatest glory that we met their leader in Jerusalem – the Grand Mufti, Sheik Muhammed Said Al-Jamal. He received us graciously and we felt a certain awe in his presence and an aura around his person.

He wore a brown galibir; nothing special about that. He wore a purple and white fez; dignified, but nothing really special about that either. The dignity was his own. It came from within. And it showed in his big, kindly Father Christmas face. His long white beard, crinkly and wavy, groomed as a horse's mane, could not hide a beaming smile. His face, lined and craggy, as if it was carved out of a great tree trunk, gave the impression of a man concerned with things eternal.

"You are welcome to this Holy Place," he began. "Think of yourselves as at the centre of the world." And then he spoke of Allah's will that there should be peace, justice for all men. And that, even if there was not peace and justice, there would always be his mercy. Man's follies could destroy their own well being but not Allah's gracious mercy. And then he outlined some of the injustices which his people currently suffered. "How can they (the occupying army) take our land and say they come to bring peace?" He said his people were forced to emigrate, to escape, to flee in any direction. Tens of thousands had crossed the river to Jordan. Many thousands had moved North to Lebanon, and now could not be traced. None could tell how many had gone to USA, from which they did not return. "But what can my people do, when their homes can be blown up and destroyed forever, on grounds of suspicion alone? The Israelis speak peace and put a gun in your ribs. They speak peace and blow up your home. They cry 'peace' where there is no peace." But Allah loved justice and would have his way. "We await His deliverance."

In answer to a question, he spoke of the shame of Moslem divisions. The religion Khomenei had inflicted on Iran was "a threat to Islam as much as it is a threat to anyone else. It is an evil on the face of the earth. It has put the arm of the sword in the place of the heart of love." And then he returned to his sad and gentle refrain "Without love, there is nothing."

However, he saw hope. Not in the present political situation. But in the hearts of men. He believed that "The I which is inside me, is the same as the 'I' which is inside you." And he was confident that in the end man's common seeking for peace and justice would enable "hearts to speak to hearts, across the boundaries of nations and religions because Allah is in the heart and the face of all the earth." He concluded "Every man, however poor, every man, however dirty, carries within him the face of our Beloved God."

"And without love – there is nothing."

We emerged into the blazing sunlight, somewhat subdued.

Later, when we talked together, we realised that there is more that unites Christians and Moslems than divides us. It was also clear that Moslems were in the midst of their own divisive conflicts and that the holy and mystical tradition of the Sufis should be heartily supported before it is overwhelmed by the militant madness of others. Our own fear of Islam often prevents this, so we have to sort ourselves out before we can be of much use.

As we left the holy place, we came across about twenty boys playing football. The ball was flat and didn't bounce and the goalposts were coke cans. But there on this most Holy Site, between the Golden Dome and the Al Aqsa Mosque, a spot sacred to Moslem, Jew and Christian and fought over for centuries, boys were playing football and laughter was in the air. It was a refreshing and cheering sign of hope, at least to me.

Tuesday, 27th October 1987

ARCHBISHOP JEJAWI of the SYRIAN ORTHODOX

It was a short walk from the Dome of the Rock and the Al Aqsa mosques, through the market stalls and jostling crowds, to the Church of John Mark. Here our second 'Father Christmas' of the morning welcomed us. He was made for the part; red robes, flowing white beard and strong smiling face. He was the Archbishop of the Syrian Community and his church was built over the traditional site of John Mark's home. The Syrians claim that their church marks the site of The Last Supper, that it was the place where the disciples hid after the crucifixion "for fear of the Jews" and that, forty days later, it was the site of the first Pentecost. The old Syriac language is close to the Aramaic of Jesus and is preserved in their liturgy so when the Archbishop read the narrative of the Last Supper we were hearing the words of Jesus in the language of Jesus.

However, it was when we asked questions that he left his written script and spoke with emotion about the painful experience of living in a divided land. "Forty years ago, I was ordained in this Church," he said. "Then there were 800 Syrian Orthodox families in Jerusalem. Now there are 20". He explained that the confiscation of land, the demolition of homes, the taxing of wealth, the power of the Israeli Occupier made normal life impossible. "Those who could go, have gone," he said. "Many to the United States. Only the old are left here." He saw very little hope in the situation, though the 'remnant' continued to worship every day and they continued to possess a small part of the Church of the Holy Sepulchre. The sadness of his story was evident to all, which made it all the more amazing that his Father Christmas face shone so brightly. Optimism outweighs realism, it is the only way the oppressed survive. The Archbishop's story partly explained why their chapel in the Holy Sepulchre was such an impoverished mess, but there was a further reason. From the earliest Councils of the Church in the fifth century, the Syrians had been condemned as 'heretical' and had therefore faced condemnation and persecution from 'orthodox', ever since. They did not dare leave anything of value in their tiny chapel for fear that it would be stolen or destroyed, even though their heresy was fifteen hundred years ago! And so, when they worshipped in the Church of the Holy Sepulchre, they brought all their finery with them, and then took it away again to the safety of their own Church of John Mark.

When we were preparing to leave, the Archbishop said, quite suddenly, "Would you like me to sing?" and, while we were considering a reply, he told us he had translated Martin Luther King's "We shall overcome" into Aramaic. "We have a lot to overcome," he said, "and so we use it like an anthem in church and we hum it at home."

Was this really the place where Jesus washed his disciples' feet on the last night of his life? The place where the disciples, hidden for fear, first heard of the resurrection? The place where, forty days later, every man heard the wonderful works of God, each in his own tongue?

As we heard a modern message of hope for a new generation of beleaguered Christians sung with fervour by an old man in an ancient language, it seemed very likely. And the wonderful works were continuing, however small the remnant.

Tuesday, 31st October 1987

MR. BASSAM SHAKKAR, Mayor of Nablus

We had been warned that the meeting with Mr. Shakkar might be difficult. For one thing, he was severely handicapped and was often confined to a wheelchair, and on 'bad days' he was not always available. For another thing, his Nablus home was surrounded by barbed wire and electronic devices and, although double steel doors added to his protection, we would not be admitted if there was a security scare at the time.

In fact, he stood at the doorway to welcome us himself, with a big smile and the cheery wave of a walking stick. In the best tradition of Arab hospitality, we were well refreshed as we heard his story.

He had farmed in the Nablus region all his working life and he had no ambition to do anything else. But all was changed in 1967 by the Six Day War. The Israeli Occupation which followed led to the confiscation of his land and his farming life was at an end. In the following years the Israelis ruled by Martial Law, with sporadic violent resistance by the occupied Palestinians. Eventually, in 1979, the Israelis decided to allow the principal occupied cities (Nablus, Ramallah and Bethlehem) to elect their own Mayor and he had been elected for Nablus. It was a poisoned chalice because he was answerable to the Israeli military for any rebellion or resistance by his own people. This gave him Palestinian enemies. The mayors of Ramallah and Bethlehem were facing similar dilemmas until it all came to and end, on

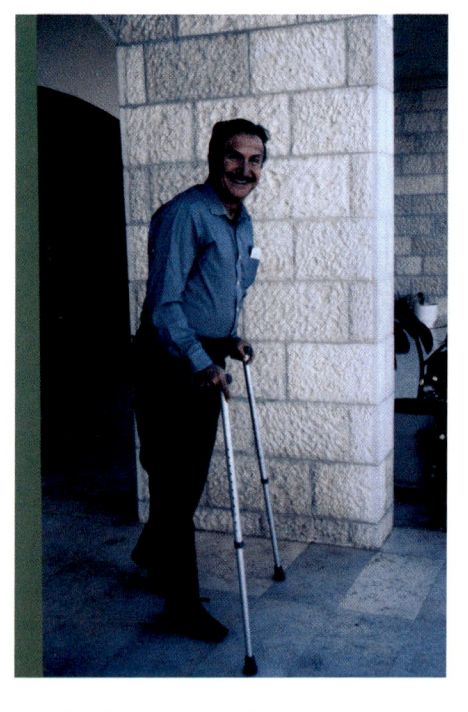

6th June 1982.

On that day, the cars of all three mayors were blown up by Jewish terrorists. The mayor of Bethlehem was killed. The mayor of Ramallah was blinded. And both legs of Bassam Shakkar were blown off. The Jewish terrorists were arrested, tried, found guilty and sentenced to five years imprisonment. They were released after three years, (less than some Palestinian youths have spent in prison for throwing stones) and Mr. Shakkar was flown to London for specialist treatment. He was there for six months while artificial limbs were fitted and he learnt to walk again.

Meantime, back in the West Bank, the Israelis decided to end the experiment of elected mayors and they appointed a new Mayor of Nablus in succession to Mr. Shakkar. The people, in a fit of fury at losing their electoral rights, decided the Israeli-nominated mayor was a collaborator and assassinated him. The Israelis then arrested a great many of Mr. Shakkar's family and friends, on suspicion of the murder. Meantime, the people of Nablus decided to hold their own elections and Mr. Shakkar had been the overwhelming victor, in spite of the fact that he was mostly confined to a wheelchair and was still learning to walk. The Israeli response was to declare his election null and void, to depose him and re-assert Martial Law. That was the present situation. The Palestinian people regarded him as their rightful chosen leader, but the power was with the Israeli militia. Hence the high security fences, the double steel doors and the electronic warning systems.

We asked him how he saw the future. "I am sorry for the Israeli," was his surprising reply. "Their policy is destroying themselves. Every time they hit us, they build our pride and our determination. The Palestinian people have never been so proud of their identity." We asked him how he coped with his severe handicap. "I am proud of it," he said, "all our people have suffered in the occupation. Some have lost sons, some have lost fathers, most have lost land, many have lost their wealth. I have lost my legs. If I had not got the mark of suffering, I could not lead a suffering people." When asked about terror as a tool, he said "We can never win an armed struggle. We have nothing, they have everything. Killing will only cause more killing. It is useless. But sometimes despair drives people to madness. It is hard to see a solution. We have had 20 years of oppression and occupation. It will lead to violence. But that is a counsel of despair."

For the photographs, he put his crutches on one side and we parted with smiles and kisses. "All I wanted was to tend my sheep," were his parting words.

Sunday, 1st November 1987

FATHER ELIAS CHACOUR, Melkite priest

Of all the many clergy of varied persuasions who live and move and have their being in the Holy Lands, Father Elias must be the best known. During the apartheid oppression, the South African church had Father Huddleston and then Desmond Tutu. During the Israeli occupation, the Palestinian church has had Elias Chacour. His name spread abroad with the publication of "Blood Brothers" but he was already known in the land because of his determination to hold Jews and Palestinians together, in spite of all their bitter conflicts. "We share the same father – Abraham – and the same God," was the teaching of his own father, even after he and his family had been violently expelled from their village and had forfeited their homes to the Zionists. Later, he developed his "Blood Brothers" theme. "This land, this Palestine, this Israel does not belong to either Jews or Palestinians. Rather we belong to the land and to each other. If we can not live together in the land, we will certainly be buried together in the land."

Elias Chacour had been born in the hill district of Galilee, in the village of Biram, where he had spent his childhood until the day their village was destroyed and they were made homeless. Today he is still in the same Galilean hill district, the parish priest in the village of Ibillin, which is where we went to meet him.

As it was Sunday, he was about to celebrate the Eucharist in a crowded church. It is my habit to ask the priest whether or not we can receive the Sacrament, when we are visitors, and so I approached him. "Excuse me, we are Anglicans," I said. "No," he replied, "you look like human beings to me." It was the sharp sword-like speech of the prophet. They do not waste words, they say significant things with brevity, but memorably. He could see my surprise, so he added "There is one qualification for the Kingdom of God : to be a human being." Knowing the strict teaching of the Pope on the issue of inter-communion, I was surprised and my face must have shown it. "Of course," he said "Unity has happened here, who can separate the children of God?" I replied that the rules wouldn't allow it, in England. "Rules? Rules? What are rules but the shackles of love. Here we have set aside rules in a greater cause."

After the service, we gathered with the congregation to break the fast and it was question time. I asked about politics. His face, masked by black beard and black hat pressed to his eyes, could not hide the tension and the anguish, and his voice changed. "There is hardness overcoming the hearts of the people. There is fear growing on both sides. Once the Palestinians were a laughing people. Only bloodshed lies ahead. Then tears." It was the plain speech of prophecy. There was a Biblical tone to his voice. I asked why things were so much worse. "In the Lebanon our brothers have been humiliated. Reduced to poverty, imprisoned in camps, they have killed their dogs for food, then they have eaten rats. Famine degrades. Humanity is destroyed. When we are de-humanised, there is no hope. The victors think they have won. But they too have been de-humanised. They too are losers. that is why the future holds only bloodshed and tears – there is no winner, only losers."

I asked what he had learnt from his travels as a speaker in United States, Britain and other places of political influence. "I only met one man who understood from the inside. Many were kind and sympathetic and wished me well. Only one man understood from the inside, Bishop Desmond Tutu of South Africa. He had said:

> 'The Palestian Plight is worse
> than that of black South Africans.
> In my country, they want us to remain
> as the white man's slaves.
> In your country, they do not even want you to remain.'

After the meal, the local people, speaking a mix of English and Arabic, took us round the church compound so that we could see the school they had built with their own hands, Christian, Moslem and Jew, working together. Five hundred children from eighteen Galilean villages attended the school which had risen from destruction and despair to become a sign of reconstruction and hope.

This is the land of the One who was 'The Hope of All Nations," said Father Elias, when he came to see us off. "He lived and walked in these hills," he said. "We must express this hope in these hills. That is why the school was built by people whose homes had been destroyed, whose sons had been killed. That is why the school is open to Christian, Moslem and Jew. That is why we learn to speak Hebrew, Arabic, English. That is why the Altar is open to all human beings. We are all children of God," and with that he waved us off. Thank God for a prophetic word, midst the gathering gloom.

Tuesday, 3rd November 1987

DAVE the POLITICAL HISTORIAN

My life-long failed romance with journalism and my other love affair, with the Middle East, made it doubly interesting to meet Dave, a political historian, who was working as a journalist for a Palestinian publication. It seemed to me that he had the job I could only dream about. He had joined our group for the week because he was "looking for stories". He had certainly found them at the Bethlehem murder and the Gaza house demolition, and so it was natural to ask him how he would report them.

But, as he told his story, it became clear that his job had problems. He had to cope with Israeli censorship. A Palestinian publication could only appear if licenced by the Israeli occupiers. In his time with the magazine, he had written seven articles. Two had been totally rejected by the Israelis so that the magazine (which was not allowed to appear with blank spaces which revealed censorship) had been obliged to reprint old articles. Two other pieces had been cut so drastically that he felt they were 'gutted and worthless'. Only one piece had been accepted, as written. In one article, he had used information and statistics already published by the Israeli Authorities – even his comment had been limited to reporting what the Israelis had already printed. But his effort had been banned. When his Palestinian editor had complained that the information was already known, he had been told "yes, but not in the Occupied Territories".

It was not only censorship they had to contend with. Their offices were subject to Police raids, at any time. Files, documents, tapes could disappear overnight. He had to write under an adopted name and he carried names addresses and telephone numbers in his head, rather than commit them to paper. Perhaps his was not a dream job after all, but I still wanted to know how he would report the Bethlehem and Gaza events.

To my dismay, he thought he would have to wait and see the Israeli papers first, even though they had not been eye-witnesses, and he had. If he wrote the true, accurate eye-witness account, it would be censored and it would compromise anyone whose comments he printed. In journalists' terms, he faced the ultimate frustration. He had two genuine 'scoops' (if death and destruction can be reduced to scoops) and he couldn't use either of them.

His dilemma as a journalist for a Palestinian publication seemed to be in sympathy with all that we had been hearing from legal bodies, University staff and religious leaders – truth was being hidden at every level. Courts were hearing false confessions, forced by brutality; schools and Universities could teach only the history, politics and philosophy approved and printed by the State. And the press was muzzled.

So it was quite a sensation when we picked up the Israeli "Jerusalem Post" (2nd Nov) and read the bold front page headline about their own Secret Police : **"SHIN BET LIED FOR 16 YEARS"**. Then followed a detailed account of the findings of a Commission of Enquiry. It acknowledged beatings, violence to suspects, illegal treatment of prisoners, false arrest, false evidence and 'widespread perjury ever since 1971'. It acknowledged that their procedures and practice had been outside International law and of a criminal nature. These were clear statements and a vindication of all the conclusions we were reaching from our own fact finding.

But the sting was in the tail. The Commission recommended no action be taken retrospectively against those who had done criminal acts "in the service of the State". The Report also recommended that new guidelines for treatment of prisoners and methods of interrogation should be "privately agreed" between the Secret Police and the government, and that 'discretion of method' should rest with the interrogator.

No wonder the leaders of Shin Bet greeted the report with "an enormous sigh of relief" and the conviction that they could now "get back to business".

The report had found them guilty but given them the freedom to carry on.

And the shooting of the Bethlehem student was reported flatly without any comment. We knew more than the reporter. Though we were even more saddened to read that "on military orders he was buried before dawn in the presence of his parents and a muktar, in an unmarked grave".

My views of Dave and his job had to be revised. His was not the work of my dreams. It was all one long nightmare.

THE CHURCHES and CONFLICT, 1987

With the people suffering midst political and military conflict, how should the Christian church respond? As we travelled, we saw a variety of answers.

The Greek Orthodox Church in Gaza

"You are welcome," said the two priests as they received us at the door of their church. "This is the church of our Patron, Saint Porphyrus, you are welcome." There were ten of us in our group, led by a Roman Catholic lecturer. "Thank you," our leader said, "we would like to begin with prayer." "No, no, that is not possible," said the priest. "This is a holy place. This is an ancient foundation. Only Orthodox prayers allowed," and he started to tell us the life story of Porphyrus whose perfectly preserved shrine was there for all to see, surrounded by a hundred lighted candles.

The two priests were immaculately clothed, their black cassocks positively shone in the candlelight, as if they had been polished. When they moved the impression given was that they were floating, or perhaps on wheels, so smooth was their movement. Their jet-black hair was tied in a bun at the back and it also shone so that the total effect was almost unearthly. Were these beings human or divine? Were they flesh and blood, like ourselves? Or were they of another order?

While we were pondering these things, the first priest said "You may sit." So we sat. The other priest, who had long fingers and manicured nails, came to our leader. "Do not cross your legs," he said. "This is not our tradition, it is an insult to God." So we uncrossed our legs and sat up straight, feeling a little like naughty children in an old-fashioned school. "You may ask questions," said the first priest.

"What work do you do in Gaza, among the refugees?" one of our number asked, which was probably the question on all lips.

"We keep out of politics," said the priest with the long fingers. "We offer the Divine Liturgy and stay close to God," said the other priest who, according to the ladies, had scented hair.

We had no doubt that the Divine Liturgy would be offered with a perfection in keeping with the shining building and the immaculate priests. After all, the distinctive offering of the Greek tradition is that their worship leads to the gate of heaven. The trouble was that outside the polished perfection was Gaza City which many would call the gate of hell. And there the people were being "crushed like grasshoppers", to use the Israeli Prime Minister's own words. It seemed that those cries from the human heart were not the concern of the Orthodox Church of Gaza. Their concern was to "stay close to God."

Our puzzle, as we left the highly polished priests behind, was how to be 'close to God' in a hellhole like Gaza.

The Roman Catholic church in Gaza

At the 'Latin' church, we were greeted by a wiry little man with wild hair and a worn cassock, once black but now grey and threadbare. We thought he was a rather run-down verger, but he turned out to be the priest. In the church there were a number of people sitting with their backs to the wall and looking as dishevelled as the priest. "When they are frightened, they take sanctuary here," said the priest. "Some stay all night, longer if their home has been bulldozed." "Doesn't it make a mess?" said one of our party. "Yes, of course, we live in a mess, Gaza is a mess, the church can not escape it. We are in it, with the people. We clear shit out of this place every morning. Come and meet the Sisters."

Mother Theresa's 'Sisters of Charity' welcomed us and took us to the 'rooms' where they worked. So many children, hopelessly deformed, or terminally diseased, lay on mattresses. With minimal medication available, they were doomed to die. So many old people, lying in dark corners some silently accepting their fate, others crying out pitifully. The whole scene could have been straight out of one of Hogarth's engravings of the bestial horrors of 18th century London. The smell and the screams were too much for most of us and several left quickly.

When the Sisters brought us tea, I asked one of them how she could embrace people who smelt so awful, and dribbled. "To us, each one is Christ," was her reply.

We left, rather hurriedly, with another view of how to be 'close to God' in Gaza.

The Anglican church in Nazareth

The Anglican cathedral in Jerusalem had disappointed us. It seemed to be caught up in its own conflicts. On the one hand it was trying to raise £180,000 to install a new organ which was being shipped in from Germany, on the other hand it was trying to minister to the impoverished Arab speaking Palestinian congregation which was steadily diminishing in number. And then there was the Pilgrim Problem. On any Sunday the Palestinian faithful might be boosted by a hundred Japanese, or bus loads of Kenyans or American visitors from a Mediterranean cruise. Or by all three. Or by none at all. How difficult to prepare the sermon, and liturgy, not knowing who to expect!

So the Cathedral had problems of its own and there was no visible sign that it ever reached beyond its own survival to grapple with the catastrophes that surrounded it. Besides, its ministry was also to Pilgrims and most Pilgrims want to be warmed with thoughts of Jesus, not shocked by stories of poverty, homelessness and injustice, even though Jesus experienced those things in the Gospel. The cathedral and its staff were cloistered. The prophetic voice would not come from there.

So when we arrived in Nazareth to visit the Anglican church, our expectations were not high. We were especially doubtful about Nazareth because we knew that a huge Jewish development on the surrounding hills had made a second city, rivalling the old city which Christians and Moslems had shared for generations. We wondered, like Nathaniel in the Gospel, whether any good thing would come out of Nazareth.

The Vicar, Canon Riah Abu El-Assal, a small and active man who was going bald and reminded me of St. Paul, greeted us with enthusiasm. He took us first to his church school which had 300 pupils, Moslem and Christian, together. Such was the school's reputation, an additional floor was being added to accommodate another 100 pupils and to add further grades to the school. The work was being done by local labour, aided by 50 young folk from 14 nations who had given 60 summer days to the project. It was hugely impressive. Something good was coming out of Nazareth.

Next we were taken to a block of 14 flats, brand new and occupied by Church families. In fact the Canon had vacated his Vicarage and moved into one himself. Another block was planned, such was their popularity. All had been built on the cooperative principle, with Church money, in an effort to raise morale and stem the tide of emigration and the despair which leads to violence.

Before long, we were viewing a block of houses – including the former Vicarage – which had been given to the Church a hundred years earlier. These were already accommodating the offices of the 'Prisoners' Aid association', and other relief organisations. "Administration has to be transparent," said the Canon. "When big money is involved in a poor country, everyone fears corruption. We must be clean."

Lastly, and most spectacularly, we were taken to the top of the mountain and shown all the kingdoms of the earth – or so it seemed. The view stretched from the Mediterranean coast to the Galilean hills from Mount Gilboa to Armageddon. This was the site of a former home for the handicapped and was now being restored, renovated and converted, most imaginatively, into a hostel which would fulfil every Pilgrim's dream. No one living, or visiting here would ask Nathaniel's question. It was evident something very good was coming out of Nazareth.

However, things were not as straightforward as they seemed. We imagined that Canon Riah's vision might have made him something of a hero. No so. The confused politics meant he faced three sets of hostile enemies.

First, a large number of Nazarenes, angry at the huge Jewish development, had formed an aggressive Communist party. The City Council was divided and, as Riah was a founder of the Democratic Front, he found himself torn apart by the factions. He supported so many of the Communist aims, but not the methods. He was caught in a political crossfire which threatened his life.

Secondly, in his Diocese, moves had twice been made by the Synod to silence him. The opposition came chiefly from the hierarchy. There were parts of the Diocese where the Clergy and people did not live under occupation or oppression, where torture, shootings and house demolitions were not problems. These Clergy wanted to silence Canon Riah's clear and outspoken rejection of Israeli occupation and his equally clear support of the P.L.O. They feared they would be black-listed and that the work of the Institutional church would be undermined.

Canon Riah with the author

And finally, predictably, the Israelis also sought his life. He was under Restriction. This meant he was not allowed to leave the country and all his lecturing and fund raising in USA and England had been forced to stop. It meant he was not allowed to travel, even to his friends or family anywhere in the Occupied territories of the West Bank. It meant his home and telephone were bugged, his mail arrived via the Intelligence, and his home, study and offices were subject to frequent Police investigation. He had been detained many times, but always released – partly because there were no grounds for any charge but mainly because of the international exposure the Israelis would have to face if he was brought before a Court.

All this was because he constantly spoke out clearly about illegal beatings, false trials, unjust confiscation of land, breach of International Law, and the right of the Palestinian people to self determination in their own land. And, to back the words, the school was being enlarged, the offices extended, the homes built and the hostel prepared.

In Nazareth we had seen works to admire, in an Occupied Land. But we had also seen the price of prophecy.

Note: Canon Riah was elected Bishop in 1996.

Bishop Riah Abu-el-Assal, pictured in 2003 at his Jerusalem Cathedral

THE CHURCHES and POLITICS, 2002

Something very sinister is happening in the land called Holy, and it is not only the violent cycle of assassinations, suicide bombings, reprisals, home demolitions and all the other horrors we have become accustomed to. There is a frightening polarisation of the chief players. And the churches have become part of it.

The Churches

It was the third week in January, the Week of Prayer for Christian Unity, observed all over the world but nowhere with quite the significance it has in Jerusalem. There is no other place in Christendom in which the principal church (The Holy Sepulchre) is shared by so many ancient churches – Greek, Armenian, Latin, Coptic, Syrian and Ethiopian – and visited by so many others. Neither is there any place in Christendom with such a history of unholy division and open hostility, each against the other, even to the extent of court cases, murder charges and continuing conspiracies; which is why the keys have to be held by a Moslem family, independent of the religious wrangling.

So it came as a welcome surprise in the week of Christian unity to find each of the ancient churches, with the exception of the Greeks, hosting the others at a series of evening services – the Anglican cathedral first, followed by the Latin (Roman) and the Armenian Patriarchates, the Coptics and the Lutherans. And at all the social gatherings which followed the prayers, one thing was clear. The dreadful circumstances in which all were seeking to survive was doing more to unite them in a common purpose than all the years of theological debate and joint reports had ever done. Old hostilities were being laid aside because there was a new and greater threat – the Israelis and the continuing Occupation, now in its fourth decade.

The stories of the Occupation were dreadful to hear. At the Armenian seminary the news was that an Arab home had been bulldozed to the ground that day, the 84th demolition in two weeks; the military had arrived at 4.00 a.m. and given the family 30 minutes to clear out. "They do this every day," said a French catholic nun. "Do you wonder they turn to terror?"

159

At the Latin Patriarchate we heard that the Archbishop of Canterbury was in Alexandria meeting with Jewish and Moslem clerics, seeking an Inter-Faith approach to the problem and the resulting violence. An Italian Franciscan denounced the initiative as a political move by Tony Blair, obediently executed by his Archbishop (Carey). It was no more than a device to get some leading Moslems 'on-side' for Blair's 'war against terror'. There was no confidence that good would come of it.

At the Lutheran reception, the pessimism was even more profound. "The problem is on the street. While rabbis in synagogues use the Sabbath to proclaim that the land is theirs by Divine Right, and while imams in the mosques rant and rage that the injustices demand Holy war, there will not be peace on the street." A Syrian elder explained that "Forgiveness is seen as weakness, revenge as strength" in popular Jewry, "and Moslems believe turning the cheek is ridiculous." It was a cocktail for disaster, and the disaster was all around us.

It was surprising to hear that the three Patriarchs – Greek Orthodox, Armenian and Roman Catholic – with the Anglican dean and others had travelled, all together, to Ramallah to greet Yassir Arafat in his beleaguered compound, surrounded by Israeli tanks. He had been refused permission to go to Bethlehem and take his traditional place at the Christmas Mass in the Church of the Nativity, so, as a sign of solidarity, all the Christian leaders had gone to him.

The sudden signs of Christian unity could be interpreted in two ways. It could be a welcome answer to years of prayer, or it could be an ominous sign of the political polarisation that is paralysing the people.

Israeli Politics

"Wherever you find two Israelis, you will find three political arguments" is one of Israel's own favourite sayings. Freedom of speech and an influx of Jews from the ex-Communist regimes of Eastern Europe, from the monarchies and republics of North Africa and from all parts of the Middle East have led to a proliferation of political parties of every hue and many temperaments.

Add to that the Religious parties with Biblical fundamentalism as their inspiration and the Torah as their manifesto and there is every likelihood of a divided Parliament. In fact it has been so divided for so long that leaders trying to form an effective Government have often had to court very small religious parties. This has frequently passed the balance of power to minority groupings that represent no more than one per cent of the people and yet can achieve their own way, or failing that, bring down the government.

Now, under Ariel Sharon, this has changed. Facing the threat of Palestinian revolt and the new wave of suicide bombings, he has brought together a Government of National Unity. A remarkable coalition of the secular and the religious parties, previously hostile to each other, and of the left and right parties (Labour and Likud) now working together, have one common purpose. To crush the Palestinian uprising.

The new political union, like the togetherness of the churches, is both an achievement and an alarming sign of polarisation.

Palestinian Politics

Palestinian politics is shrouded in secrecy and hidden from public view. This is partly because there is no Palestinian state to be governed during the Occupation, partly because the political parties had to be secretive in the days when the P.L.O. was branded as a terrorist organisation, partly because so many leaders know they may follow the fate of their colleagues and suffer assassination, partly because Palestinians can not agree among themselves on an effective response to Occupation. Armed resistance will be crushed. Urban guerrillas will receive world condemnation. Passive resistance has led them nowhere. Now added to all this confusion come radical Islamic groups from neighbouring Arab states, bringing with them the militant threats of "Hamas", "Islamic Jihad" and "Hezbollah". Ordinary Palestinians probably live in as much fear of these private militias as they do of the Israeli occupier. And every home which is bulldozed, every leader that is assassinated, strengthens support for the militants.

All this was made painfully clear on CNN television tonight *(Jan.21,*

2002). Following the murder of four Palestinians in Nablus, the Hamas movement (which had kept a three-week ceasefire) declared all-out war on Israel and the newsreel pictures showed Arafat applauding them, shaking hands and releasing the Hamas prisoners he had previously detained. Arafat has vacillated too long, at one time arresting and holding extremists, as the Israelis demand that he should do; at other times releasing them to return to their militias. The impression is that he has no clear and principled policy but that he constantly manoeuvres to save his own skin. The latest move, in response to his own house arrest. and the destruction of his headquarters is to look to Hamas and anyone who will come to his rescue.

So the polarisation of all parties nears completion. The Palestinian factions, so long hostile to each other, are uniting. The Israeli factions, previously in conflict, are in solid coalition. The Christian churches, after centuries of hostilities, show remarkable togetherness. But all for the purpose of facing their enemies. The scene is set for unholy battle and innocent blood will flow.

Chapter Five

The Road Map, June 2003

The Road Map

5th June 2003

The Road to Peace in the Middle East has been mapped out with a Noble Two Fold Purpose of Security for Israel and an Independent State for Palestine by 2005. That sounds good, fair and hopeful for both sides, which is just as well because there is no alternative on the table, or around the corner. That is certain because this plan is devised by the United Nations, Russia, the European Union and the United States acting together – which doesn't leave many other players to produce anything else.

The plan also has unprecedented political back-up on both sides, and internationally. The Israeli cabinet has backed Prime Minister Sharon's commitment to the process, even though it was only by a majority vote. The leadership of the Palestinian Authority backed the scheme without division and Yasser Arafat, the chairman, says that Prime Minister Abbas speaks for him and the Palestinian people. And that is not all! For the Great Launching at King Abdullah's Aqaba Palace by the Red Sea, no fewer than five Arab countries bordering on Israel/Palestine were represented by senior officials hosted by the King of Jordan. And, just in case there was a single lingering doubt, President Bush made it clear that his personal representative, Mr. John Wolf, would take up residence within a week, with a team of six to help both sides follow the map, step by step.

There can not have been such a sense of purpose or such a show of unanimity in living memory. So what's the delay? Let's get on with it! Why not tomorrow?

The Jewish 'Street'

The English language 'Jerusalem Post' has a different story to tell. Under the headline "A Recipe for Disaster", the editorial declares the 'Map' is a surrender to terrorism and that every bomber will laugh that his evil deeds have brought him the reward he wanted. Another article under the headline "The Map is a Trap" points out that one of the early steps on the road will require Israel to close and dismantle settlements. It warns that the last Israeli Prime Minister to compromise on that issue was assassinated. "The land is our God-given birthright and can never be given to terrorists, proven criminals, or anyone else. It is ours and anyone who gives it away is guilty of an act of treason, even if he is the Prime Minister."

To drive the editor's point home, street demonstrations followed under the banner "G-d is a Zionist". Ten thousand settlers gathered to march on Zion Square, strong evidence that they will not be moved 'not now, not ever' as one banner proclaimed. Another group of Orthodox demonstrators, coming from a different direction, announced that 'Jordan is Palestine', a clear indication that the only place for Palestinians is on the other side of the river, leaving the whole of Palestine's West Bank land to Israel, exclusively.

The newspaper was overwhelmed by the letters of protest and could only print a small selection. They must have chosen the more extreme : "I would rather die than see a centimetre of our beloved land pass to goiim" (gentiles). "Are we now to give in to the devils who blow up our children?" and "We want the land and we will have it, all of it, not some of it, because the Lord (Blessed be He) has given it to us."

Clearly, between the political leadership backing 'The Map' and the popular opinion on 'the street', a great gulf is fixed. Equally clearly, any ambitious politician who breaks ranks with the leadership will have an immediate following, not so much a fertile field to hoe as a ready crop to harvest.

The Arab Street

The day after Bush, Sharon and Abbas had shaken hands at Aqaba with supporting statesmen looking on, I bought a newspaper and said to the stall holder "Good news" pointing to the picture. "Pah!" he said and, taking another paper, he tore it in two and spat on the ground. Not the expected response and a less than cheerful start. A little later, at a coffee shop, the owner, speaking eloquent English, explained. "Abbas is not our man. He is Bush's 'Yes Man'. Arafat is our elected leader, not Abbas." He couldn't understand why the Americans talk about democracy but reject the democratic choice of the Palestinians and choose another. "No one will follow Abbas. Even the people who doubted Arafat will support Arafat now: The Americans don't understand that."

The television news was equally discouraging. The three main military factions which Abbas had hoped would support a cease-fire said that without doubt, they wouldn't. They went even further. They said that Abbas had gone too far at the Road Map launching in saying the Intifada had been a mistake. "Is he saying our sons have wasted their lives?" And he had not gone far enough in urging an end to the Occupation. "We will continue the armed struggle until every part of Occupied Palestine is free," they concluded, to great cheers.

That day it took four hours to drive the seven miles to Bethlehem. The checkpoint was closed we were told, "the wall blocks everything." Then we were told another checkpoint was open, but it could be closed by the time we got there. When we did get there, the crowd, all caged, was too large to join. "Is this the Road Map?" someone shouted at me. And the message was that unless things changed, quickly, on the ground, to end this daily humiliation, no one would believe the Road Map was worth a shekel.

Clearly, between the political leadership backing the 'map' and the popular opinion on the street, a great gulf is fixed.

Equally clearly, the militias of Hamas and Islamic Jihad have a huge and virile crop of frustrated youngsters, ready for harvest.

Civil War in Israel?

Israel boasts that its new population is drawn from 70 countries on every Continent of the globe. In this small land sophisticated Europeans and poorly-educated North Africans, wealthy Americans and impoverished Ethiopians, highly skilled Russians and unskilled South Americans live alongside, as neighbours. Some are secular citizens who reject religious culture, others are Orthodox Jews who control and direct the law and the customs of the majority; many are exempt military service on religious grounds, which annoys those whose military service protects them. It is said that wherever two Jews meet, there are three political opinions. It is also said that the ultimate Divine Punishment would be to give them the land, so that they had to live with each other.

The Israeli nation must be the most varied mix ever brought together in the world's colourful history. Some say the only thing which holds them together and gives them common purpose is the Palestinian presence. They can agree on one thing, if on nothing else – the Arabs are the common enemy.

So what will happen if an Israeli government makes a compromise which accepts that Palestinians will have full rights to part of the land? What will happen if an Israeli government which has subsidised the settlers, now orders them out of the settlements? What will the Religious powers do if they see their Government surrendering the land that they believe is theirs by Divine Right?

The last time this happened, the Religious Right assassinated the Prime Minister and the killer became a hero. If the Road Map is implemented, it is difficult to see how Israel will avoid an explosion of civil strife on a much greater scale. Many Israelis hope that the Palestinians kill the Road Map, before Israel has to meet its obligations and face the internal violence which would surely follow.

Civil War among Palestinians?

Palestinians never agreed on how to respond to the founding of the State of Israel in the first place, or on the Occupation of their land since 1967 and so it is no surprise that there are conflicting responses to the latest challenge, the Road Map.

There have always been those who thought that the military advances of Israel should be met by a military response and there have always been a well publicised number who would resist the oppression of Occupation by any means. Violence has been part of the opposition to Israel's military control, from the beginning.

Equally, there has always been a less publicised number who have seen that there could be no military solution because the scales were hopelessly weighted in favour of a highly sophisticated military machine with unlimited American training, equipment and financial backing. There could be but one winner, and it wouldn't be the Palestinian. These favoured dialogue or passive resistance but neither could show any progress for their efforts, with the result that an ever-increasing number turn to guerrilla tactics, or terror as it has become known.

So the sorry circuit of Occupation, Resistance, Punishment, has taken hold. Those who seek to break it by a return to dialogue and negotiation are scorned as weaklings. Militant Islamists come from other Arab states to help, but clash with the Palestinian people, many of whom privately fear Militant Islam.

If the Road Map is implemented, who will control the infant Palestinian state? Will it become an Islamic state like neighbouring Saudi Arabia? a secular state like neighbouring Egypt? Will Syria expect to be rewarded for its solid support? Will the United States expect to establish a puppet government? It is hard to see how a new State will be established without a torrent of blood-letting in which the innocent will continue to suffer.

The Christian Situation

The presence of the Holy Places makes the conflict between Israelis and Palestinians even more complicated. For two thousand years, there has been an unbroken Christian presence in the land, so much so that all over the world it is known as 'The Holy Land' as much as it is known as Israel or as Palestine. The Christian faith has its human origins in the Jews and Arabs present at the first Pentecost and its geographical origins throughout the land. The land's destiny is of utmost concern to Christians, and the Road Map, or any other path to Peace, could bring blessings, but could bring a curse and a catastrophe.

The blessings are so obvious that they don't need detailing. To come and go in peace, to move freely from place to place, to see justice done for those who have been deprived of home and land, to see Jew and Arab living without fear as good neighbours, these are blessings not only for Christians but for people of goodwill all over the world.

The curse and the catastrophe which could befall the Christians does need detailing because it is not widely understood. Too often, people think of Christians and the Holy Land in terms of pilgrims and visitors – vast numbers from every nation under heaven – whose total experience of the land will be the ten days or fortnight of their flying visit. The indigenous Christians, born here and with no other place to go, are overlooked.

The number of indigenous Christians has fallen by 80% since the State of Israel was founded. The Arab Christians have suffered a fate similar to all the other Palestinians. They have lost homes and land, they have fled to Jordan and other Arab states, they have emigrated to any country which would have them. Those remaining tend to be the elderly and are so few in number that they are certainly the vulnerable. In a new and independent State, it is doubtful the Christian voice or vote would be of much significance. They would form a minority group, and a small one. While under Israeli Occupation, they are victims alongside all the other victims, in an Independent State they could easily be seen as strangers and aliens in a Moslem dominated land. No one knows the form an Independent State would take.

Under Arafat (whose wife is a Christian) it would be a secular State and the Christians would continue to be valued. The present rapport between all the Christian churches and Arafat is surprisingly good. His prime place as 'President' is still reserved in the Church of the Nativity at the Christmas Midnight Eucharist, even though he can not escape his Ramallah house arrest to be there. Christians and Moslems have shared their life together for centuries, attending each other's Festivals, especially in the villages. And of course it is a Moslem family which holds the keys of the Holy Sepulchre.

Under Sheik Yassin, the promoter of Jihad and the 'spiritual' leader of the military resistance (terror, in western language) the Constitution of an

Independent State would be Islamic and the place of minorities could not be guaranteed. He would gather support from other revolutionary elements, especially the Iranian and the Saudi. The prospects for the Christians and for the Christian sites could be catastrophic.

Is There a Way Ahead?

Will the Road Map, after it has taken early knocks from both sides, settle down and become the accepted way ahead?

In the absence of any other scheme, there are two alternatives. One is the continuation of the present horrors, - fear for Israelis, open prison for Palestinians, broken economy for both. The other alternative is war.

The Second World War arose out of the settlement of the First, which punished the Germans with such unbearable burdens that it gave birth to German nationalism and the rise of Hitler. The next world war is already arising from the unjust settlement of the last one, which punished Arabs for all that Europeans had done to the Jews. This has given birth to the massive Arab resentment and resistance which we call terrorism.

The Third World War has begun. It is already happening. It is different from previous wars because the combatants are not identifiable nation states and the weapons are not conventional arms. The war, dubbed 'against terror' is against an unseen enemy whose only hope of success is to remain hidden and to strike stealthily.

The powerful and highly visible U.S. war machine, led by a born-again Christian, seems to think that hitting hard with military might will destroy this terror. They fail to realise that every time they hit hard, with every bomb they drop, every time they clamp down on 'terror' they push the moderates into the arms of the militants. The present military excursions do more than any terror to bring about the very sort of Islamic state most feared. The folly was painfully exposed by the boast of an American general who, when we asked how the problems could be solved, answered us with pride, "Americans don't solve problems. We annihilate them." It is the wrong way ahead.

The 'War against Terror' is a mistaken war. The war conducted by the wealthy U.S. and allies should be a campaign against the causes of terror. A campaign for clean water where there is none and for basic education so that ignorance no longer draws youngsters into fundamentalism, would be a quarter the cost of military exploits, would make friends instead of enemies, all over the world. That is the right way ahead, that is a Road Map all would follow.

And the Holy Land? If America were seen to be using its wealth in these ways, and laying aside its killing machine, it is just possible it might be trusted as a fair broker instead of feared as a one-sided partisan.

Postscript

How to make a Terrorist
in three easy lessons

First, TAKE HIS LAND

- 72% of the West Bank has been declared 'Israeli state land' and confiscated from Palestinians without compensation
- 400,000 Israelis have settled in the expropriated land, destroying the olive groves which were the source of employment and income

Palestinian loss of land, 1946 - 1999
Maps by Palestine Solidarity Campaign

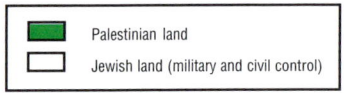

Palestinian land
Jewish land (military and civil control)

"The International community does not recognise Israel's sovereignty over any part of the occupied territories." (U.S. State Dept. Feb. 2001)

- 250 miles of new highways give Israeli settlers and soldiers free movement
- West Bank Palestinians are confined to 200 disconnected 'islands'

These facts are provided by the Israeli Committee against House Demolitions: 2003

"What I discovered was that a West Bank Palestinian could not work, build, study, purchase land, grow produce, start a business, take a walk at night, visit his family in Gaza, enter Israel or travel abroad without a permit from us and that we had imprisoned about one third of the entire Palestinian population." (Uri Savir, Israel's chief negotiator at Oslo)

Second, IF HE PROTESTS, BULLDOZE HIS HOME

- 2,850 Palestinian homes were demolished between the 1993 Oslo Peace Agreement and the 'Uprising' protest in September 2000.

- 1,162 Palestinian homes were bulldozed between September 2000 and November 2002. Most occupants were given an hour's notice to quit. The bulldozers usually arrived at night.

- The demolitions, illegal in International Law, are authorised by the Israeli courts as 'collective punishment' for crimes committed elsewhere and by others.

Facts supplied by Israeli Committee Against House Demolitions

> "I got a real kick out of every house that was demolished because dying means nothing to them but the loss of their house means everything. It destroys 40 or 50 people for a generation. If one thing bothers me it was that we didn't destroy the whole camp." (Zadok Yehezkeli, driver of D-9 bulldozer at Jenin 2002)

> "Over the years Israelis had cultivated a self-serving myth that ours was an enlightened occupation. Our self image as a humane society and as history's eternal victim has blinded us to what is going on in the occupied territories ..." (Uri Savir)

Photo courtesy International Solidarity Movement →

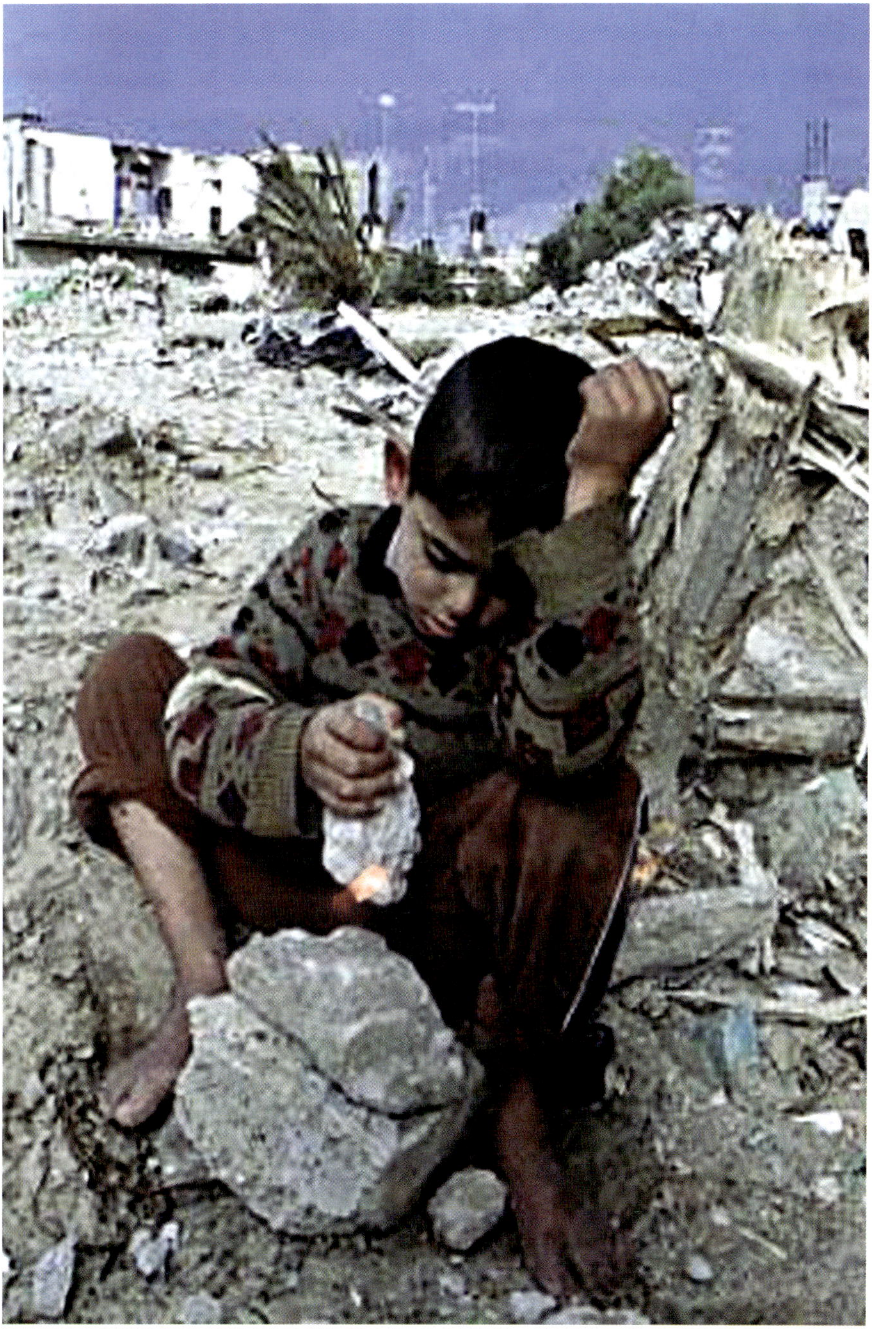

Third, IF HE STILL COMPLAINS, SEND IN THE TANKS

- US military aid to Israel is $2,068 million per year
- US unrestricted economic aid to Israel is $720 million per year
- US gifts to assist migration and settlement is $60 million per year
- US loan guarantees to Israel are $2 billion per year

   (Figures produced by Israeli Jerusalem Centre for Social and Economic Rights)

Photo Musa Alsha'er

**If your homeland was invaded
would you resist or surrender?**

**And if you resisted,
would you be a terrorist or a hero?**

The question to be faced by the Bush/Blair coalition is clear:

Is their 'War against Terror' on the right track?

Or will it create more terrorists/heroes?

There must be another way, a better way.

A campaign against the causes of terror would be a very different thing and withdrawal from Occupied Land would be the start.

"All I wanted was to tend my sheep."
(Bassam Shakkar, former Mayor of Nablus)